The Fourth Strike

Contributors

Albert D. Cunningham, Jr.
Robert H. Gudger
Stephen G. Harrison
Abner Haynes
William Watson Hines, III
Adolph Holmes
John B. Kelley
Harold W. Phend
Walter Victor Rouse
Robert E. Williams

The Fourth Strike

Hiring and Training the Disadvantaged

Edited by William D. Drennan

E 70

American Management Association, Inc.

International standard book number: 0–8144–2136–9
Library of Congress catalog card number: 74–109522

Foreword

PERSONNEL management in this country is confronted with a problem unique in its experience: the successful employment and training of America's untouchables—the hard-core unemployed. These human beings, both product and victim of neglect, lack the skills to be hired under traditional employment standards. However, they are starting to be brought onto the business scene through the use of imaginative new concepts in industrial relations. Indeed, this process has caused management to reconsider its standard employment policies for *all* employees.

In *The Fourth Strike*, our contributing authors—all of whom have had firsthand experience in this field—analyze practical aspects of this problem. Often the hard-core unemployed must be sought out—methods of doing this are discussed. The initiation, staffing, conduct, and financing of the training program are covered, including such aspects as sensitivity training, use of coaches and the "buddy system," and coordination with unions. Drunkenness, absenteeism, lateness, drug taking, and illiteracy are also probed. Emphasis has been placed on the role of medium-size or small companies; consortiums are discussed as an option for these firms.

Specific programs come and go; perhaps the ultimate value

of a book of this type lies in the realization that the affluent and advantaged and the poor and disadvantaged can learn to work together.

COLIN MACPHERSON
Manager, Personnel Division
American Management Association

Contents

Contents

The Disadvantaged:
Development of the Worker

William Watson Hines, III

THE purpose of this article is to describe the problems of the hard-core unemployed and to indicate how these problems affect them in hiring and work situations. It will outline the stresses of life in their neighborhoods and show how these factors warp their development as functioning workers. Finally, techniques will be presented whereby the disadvantaged may be recruited, successfully trained, and made effective members of the workforce.

The business community today is confronted with a growing problem: the need to devise methods that will enable it to hire and effectively use the services of those living in our inner

WILLIAM WATSON HINES, III is Senior Research Scientist—Training, The Center for the Study of the Unemployed, New York University, New York.

cities. This situation has come about as the result of a scarcity of labor available to staff the factories and offices and to run the machinery of our companies.

Most of the inner city inhabitants are blacks or poor whites who migrated from southern farm areas in the 1950s and 1960s because of mechanization. However, many arrive in the city with few or no skills to compete for jobs in an urban area. Skills acquired on a farm are of little use in a highly industrialized center. Jobs identified with the construction industry that have traditionally absorbed unskilled farm labor—for example, pick-and-shovel work and wheelbarrow labor—are handled by increasingly efficient mechanical devices. The end effect of this mechanization has been a gradual dwindling of jobs for unskilled migrants to the city. Their total has been swelled by numbers of Mexican Americans and Puerto Ricans also lacking skills needed for urban employment.

With the increased movement of these disadvantaged to the central areas of the city and the increasing exodus of the middle class to the outer city and the suburbs, many businessmen find that they must train disadvantaged workers for job openings to remain competitive.

The Ghetto Environment

The new migrants have little option but to live in run-down housing. Their finances are meager, and they have had no effective lobby to seek better conditions; many landlords refuse to make repairs or even to provide basic maintenance. Plumbing is usually in a state of complete dysfunction, adequate heat is seldom provided in the winter, hallways and staircases are ill-lighted, hot water is often not available, and roaches abound. Frequently, large holes may be found in ceilings and walls of these apartments, making perfect entryways for rats. The cycle of despair generated by the ghetto displays itself in a proliferation of scattered garbage—but garbage collection is infrequent. Much of the housing is noisy and crowded, with one bathroom shared by several families. Furniture is often scanty, and beds are sometimes shared by several members of a family. Noises from the streets and from adjacent apartments are often distracting, preventing some people from getting sufficient sleep; thus when an individual *is* employed, he may not seem to be alert enough to give an employer a full day's work. Waking up and preparing for work become far more difficult for these disadvantaged than for the middle class. However, the ghetto noise level is often so persistent and so high that some slum dwellers eventually develop a tendency to pay little or no attention to *any* sound. At the beginning of a job program, a trainee's inattention to a spoken request may be an extension of this reaction.

Many minority group members live in decaying slums because of "the familiar doublet of poverty and racial discrimination," according to the National Advisory Commission on Civil Disorders. "Poverty means they cannot pay rents or prices required for new or rehabilitated units and hence are not a market for the building industry," the Commission continued. "The same factor deters landlords from investing in maintenance of existing buildings, rendering housing codes all but unenforceable. Racial discrimination 'prevents access to many non-slum areas, particularly the suburbs,' and creates a 'back pressure' in the ghetto that increases overcrowding and boosts rent to abnormal heights."*

The ghetto residents hate the depressing room or apartment in which they are all but forced to live. Street corners or alleyways frequently become meeting places or hangouts for them to idle away time between sporadic periods of employment and to escape the oppressiveness of their living quarters. However, some men who visit the street corners or hangouts, as

* One Year Later: An Assessment of the Nation's Response to the Crisis Described by the National Advisory Commission on Civil Disorders (New York: Urban America, Inc. and The Urban Coalition, 1969), p. 47.

noted in Elliot Liebow's book *Tally's Corner*,† may work afternoons or evenings or have days off that are different from the traditional nine-to-five, Monday-to-Friday work schedule. Often they have not learned to use their leisure time constructively.

Characteristics of the Disadvantaged

The daily pressure merely to feed and clothe his family drains the energy of the underprivileged worker. His lack of training discourages him from setting career goals, and he despairs for the future of his children. During the growth and development stages, the ghetto child—who later becomes the ghetto worker—usually will not have a desire to achieve and succeed instilled in him by his family. The parents' problem of physical survival does not allow this child the opportunity to develop the ambition, the drive for new skills, and the educational achievement that are associated with the middle class.

The disadvantaged worker may not seem to be intellectually bright by middle-class standards, but he has developed a kind of "sophistication" as a result of the challenges and frustrations of his environment. In his daily effort to survive he has become hypersensitive to personal criticism, which he often considers as an attack on his manhood, and which may remind him of past rejection.

The disadvantaged worker lives in a climate of fear and suspicion. He is sensitive to being hurt. He is "living scared" and may expect rejection from management and the other workers because his experience has taught him to expect hostility from those outside his group.

From Aaron L. Rutledge and Gertrude Z. Gass's *19 Negro Men* we find that "fear is instilled into the developing personality and is regularly reinforced even when society makes some contrary effort to erase the dread and to provide fair treatment.

† Elliot Liebow, *Tally's Corner* (Boston: Little, Brown and Company, 1967), p. 15.

Individual personalities tend to become either calloused or hypersensitive as the result of being hurt through the effects of long-term discrimination."‡

The disadvantaged worker has been conditioned to develop behavior that he feels protects him from what he sees as hostile forces around him. Prevalent also are traits of a man with low self-esteem; this is shown in gross ambiguity of conduct. He develops certain peculiar survival techniques and styles—"peculiar or different dress, speech, manner, reflecting generalized hypersensitivity, a compensatory form of low threshold for aggression and hostility."§

Lack of opportunity and daily frustration, anger, and defeat also influence the worker to be cautious of those with whom he is to work. He arrives at the job site ready to be disliked or rejected by those he will encounter in the plant or office environment. His behavior seems paranoid; he has feelings of suspicion about his co-workers. Conditions in the ghetto have influenced him not to believe any "outsider" who might offer to assist him.

Elliot Liebow writes in *Tally's Corner* that "each man comes to the job with a long job history characterized by his not being able to support himself and his family. Each man carries this knowledge, born of his experience, with him. He comes to the job flat and stale, wearied by the sameness of it all, convinced of his own incompetence, terrified of responsibility. . . .

"Convinced of their inadequacies, not only do they not seek out the few better paying jobs which test their resources, but they actually avoid them, gravitating in mass to the menial, routine jobs which offer no challenge—and therefore pose no

‡ Aaron L. Rutledge and Gertrude Z. Gass, *19 Negro Men: Personality and Manpower Retraining* (San Francisco: Jossey-Bass, Inc., 1967), p. 43.

§ Kenneth B. Clark, "Ghetto Youth See Right Through Hypocrisy: 'No Gimmicks, Please, Whitey,'" *Training in Business and Industry*, November 1968, p. 27.

threat to the already diminished images they have of them-selves."¶

Ghetto-bred residents see little reason to succeed on a job. They usually will attempt to obtain the lowest-skilled and low-est-paying work. Historically, the jobs at the bottom of the lad-der have been the only ones open to them in the workforce; these jobs pose no threat to their image of themselves.

Recruiting the Hard-Core Unemployed

Nonwhites in many parts of this country have been taught that there are "white" jobs and "colored" jobs, and because of the racial practices of some state employment services that have helped to institutionalize this pattern, they expect to be treated with indifference by *any* state employment service as well as by private employment agencies. Much of the same feeling is shared by hard-core unemployed workers who in-quire about job openings or arrive for a job interview in private industry. Thus they look lightly upon advertisements and spot radio announcements that attempt to attract them to inter-views. In addition, a number of Puerto Rican and Mexican-American workers are unable to understand advertisements or announcements in English.

When the prospective worker arrives at the employment office he is often given a long application form to complete; but it is often difficult for him to do this because of his lack of for-mal education, and Mexican-American and Puerto Rican work-ers may not be able to read English. The inability to complete the form contributes to the potential worker's frustration and anxiety and adds to his general feeling of worthlessness. In ad-dition, the hard-core unemployed often must wait what seems to them an inordinately long time in the personnel office before their interview. It is important to note this, because the poten-tial worker views it as part of a rejection process that will cul-

¶ Liebow, pp. 53–54.

14

minate in his rejection for the job. He feels literally beaten down by the experience. Thus it would seem advisable for management to prepare an initial bilingual application form that asks only for basic information, and to accelerate the interview process with the disadvantaged.

Many of the disadvantaged have experienced indifferent and condescending treatment at the hands of middle-class interviewers—who might, indeed, be black. Many unemployed men and women prefer to remain in the slums rather than suffer indignities from such insensitive and discriminatory people. The in-plant interviewer should be as sensitive to the needs of the hard-core unemployed as the recruiter in the ghetto, whose function will be discussed later in this article. The problem of obtaining funds for transportation can also prevent many potential workers from appearing at the job site to ask about employment.

Traditional methods of recruiting and prescreening of the hard-core unemployed may take place through state employment services, concentrated employment programs, multiservice centers, neighborhood centers, and those Labor Department programs that have intake, counseling, screening, and referral capacities.

Additional recruitment sources are community churches, in which job announcements can be read or posted. Included in this group should be little-known churches, such as Evangelical, Pentecostal, and Spiritualist.

Local parents' associations and antipoverty agencies have knowledge of neighborhood conditions not available to those unfamiliar with life in the ghetto. Many of these agencies have offices dispersed throughout the community and are staffed with community residents. The activities of these agencies can serve as a barometer of the available workforce. Some of the agencies provide both vocational and family counseling. They can be excellent recruiting sources.

Trade schools and police community relations departments can also assist in locating the hard-core unemployed. VISTA volunteers and self-help community organizations are also good sources. Perhaps the least traditional sources, but possibly the most fruitful, are pool halls, barber shops, and local hangouts, where unemployed men spend much of their time.

Hiring of workers might best be accomplished by having a personnel representative recruit in the ghetto itself. The recruiter must be a person who is at ease with and able to relate to all types of people; one who will not attempt to affect local speech patterns; one who can talk to and respect each potential employee as a person of worth; one who will not use such words as "boy," "girl," and "you people" when addressing adults; and one who will not relate how he or she loves all blacks or Puerto Ricans or Mexican Americans, or how he loves and respects Jackie Robinson or Ralph Bunche—such an approach might be perceived as patronizing and insensitive and might well defeat management's good intentions. He should not needlessly alienate the potential worker by his questions or even by negative nonverbal expression. In short, the success or failure of this type of recruitment hinges on the ability of the interviewer to understand and communicate with the hard-core unemployed.

It should be made clear to the local residents that the firm intends to hire on the spot. Prior to this, management should devise a nonverbal testing system to evaluate the skills of the potential worker. Such a system has been successfully used by both Ford and Chrysler in hiring ghetto workers in Detroit.

In addition, management might want to examine the work sample technique developed by Jewish Employment and Vocational Services in Philadelphia. This method was developed by JEVS because it realized that many disadvantaged persons were unable to pass the traditional written test it gave to its new employees. Slum dwellers have a history of failure in school, and they fear taking written examinations. Thus their abilities might better be measured using the work sample technique, which simulates activities encountered on a regular job. Standard tools and equipment used in plant or office situations are used.

Training the Disadvantaged

Management cannot expect a worker who comes from a severely deprived social, economic, and educational environment to start working with the proper orientation toward the middle-class work environment. It should thus initiate an internal training program designed to make him a more effective worker. Industry already has training programs for executive personnel and frequently finances their participation in seminars, workshops, and conferences to aid in their development. This approach should be used for the disadvantaged worker as well, or he will be regarded by his fellow workers as a parasite rather than as an integral part of the organization.

Many businessmen have found this type of training to be administratively better than the present incentive program that is subsidized by the U.S. Department of Labor. This program provides an average of $3,500 per person per year for the hiring and training of hard-core unemployed. This incentive payment can be used in a variety of ways, including transportation costs and counseling, and prevocational training and remedial training programs. Some companies, however, have not found this approach particularly workable. In many cases, the small company either does not have the internal training capacity or is unwilling to invest in its development. Many firms maintain that their focus is on production and not on a substantial movement into the training of new workers, which they feel is excessively costly.

Management should have a continuous training program to help change the attitudes of the new worker toward the world of work—particularly regarding job rules and regulations. In order to deal with the negative expectations and behavior that might be exhibited by some of the hard core, group sessions should be conducted weekly and, when possible, on company time. Attendance should be limited to 15 or less. This small group size will encourage the less aggressive or shy worker to participate freely in the exchange and discussions. In addition, the ability to express these emotions will help to unfreeze negative feelings about the structured job situation.

Management can serve as a catalyst at these sessions by permitting the worker to reveal what is on his mind. The airing of hostile feelings among people with similar hostilities should hopefully serve a therapeutic purpose. In addition, the individual will begin to look at himself realistically in terms of where he would like to go in the business world. This type of program might be of particular value to the ghetto worker, who may for the first time have someone listen to him when he talks. Such meetings also will demonstrate that management is concerned with the problems of its disadvantaged workers and is sympathetic toward the adjustment required to make them productive employees.

Management will find it important to the success of these programs to provide a counselor to the trainees until they have successfully adjusted to the job. He can assist in handling some of the problems that may develop during the course of the day, help the trainees to better understand the demands of the business world, and act as liaison between management and the trainees.

A definite period of time should be provided early in the trainee's employment to explain the company's employee policies and the benefits available to him. Among particular items that deserve special attention are job rules and regulations, salary, frequency of pay periods, insurance and retirement plans, salary increments, sick leave, and vacation time. During this session the employee should be encouraged to ask questions about the material covered. This question-and-answer period will permit management to evaluate the effectiveness of the orientation program.

During this period, sessions on management of finances should also be included. Such a program should include items that relate to the types of establishments from which money should be borrowed; an explanation of loans, liens, garnishment, and cosigning; the use of leisure time (such as visits to museums, parks, and free exhibits); and the availability of free courses or classes in adult education. Such activities might provide the first exposure of many slum workers to activities outside their own communities. In addition, once the worker begins to make money, he will seek to buy some of the items he sees advertised. Consumer advice will help him to be more selective in his purchasing. In the long run, these sessions may reduce the man-hours lost from the job and may help to develop a more enlightened and concerned worker. I suggest that no fewer than twenty sessions be conducted, at two hours per session.

The Work Situation

Management has often promoted individuals to supervisory roles who, for the most part, are good technicians but who lack the skills to supervise and motivate workers properly. Others have been promoted only because of seniority.

In order to better prepare supervisors to work with disadvantaged employees effectively, we must provide the supervisors with special training to help them understand the outlook and attitudes of the disadvantaged. Indeed, management at all levels should be aware of these factors.

The attitudes of supervisory personnel will affect the outcome of a program to train the hard core. The supervisor's attitude will affect both the performance level and the morale of *all* his workers.

Top management should play a vital part in the success of any training program. It must not make the naïve assumption that it need not prepare the work climate for the movement of the disadvantaged into the workforce or that all its personnel fully support the new hiring policy. It is top management's responsibility to set the tone for the program. In addition, it must be involved in an ongoing program of interpretation and evaluation of the problems encountered by its personnel, and prompt in handling cases of unfavorable employee reaction, particularly when serious incidents occur. This will prevent the spread of resentment by only one or a few employees. The key to the success of such a policy lies in consistent adherence to this practice, because the disadvantaged worker will then *believe* that the company is committed to its policy and will begin to feel that he is necessary in the day-to-day operations of the firm.

Management should not lower work standards to meet the needs of the disadvantaged worker. He may interpret this to mean that management views him as inferior; in addition, such action will unfavorably affect the morale of other employees.

If we are to motivate the new worker to begin changing his behavior pattern, training in the classroom and on the job should be planned so that the trainees can begin to apply immediately, but in stages, the skills they are learning. They should be continually informed of their progress and of the steps necessary to complete particular phases in the program. Training directors will recognize that this is a need among all employees, advantaged or disadvantaged. The disadvantaged worker must be made to feel that he shares the same promotional opportunities as the other employees.

The trainee's job assignment must be one that is meaningful to him and acceptable to the rest of the workforce, or he may soon lose interest, and the other employees may become resentful. Historically, the disadvantaged worker has been assigned the most menial jobs. In addition, he is aware of a credibility gap between those who espouse a "start at the bottom—work to the top" theory and members of various minority communities who refuse to take dead-end jobs or employment that white America no longer considers desirable. On the contrary, the work assignment should be one of the regular assignments in the plant or office. A good job assignment, job security, and a good salary can be considered compensation to the new worker for the self-denial required to change his old habits and to aid him in developing such traits as punctuality, responsibility, and loyalty to job and company.

There should be members of the general workforce with whom the trainee can identify and who share his background. These should be men who have succeeded because of their ambition and work. Acquaintance with others on the workforce who have "made it" can be a deciding factor in the disadvantaged worker's own adjustment to his job. If the experiences of others have been positive, *his* attitude will be positive.

The company may need to provide the new worker with transportation to the industrial site. This is often necessary because plants and factories are generally located at great distances from slum areas, and the disadvantaged often lack even the fare when they begin a new job. The firm's recruiters should make it known that transportation will be available from the neighborhood to the business site. If the recruit is fortunate enough to have transportation, parking facilities should be provided. These approaches will lessen the trainee's anxiety during the early stages of his employment.

The company should make sure that sanitary facilities are adequate. Clean shower facilities that can be utilized before or after work may be an additional incentive for the trainee to get to work on time—some workers may not have such facilities at home, and if they are available, they might be in a state of disrepair or completely out of service. This kind of forethought alone will tell the trainee that the firm views him as an individual of worth and is concerned about his health and cleanliness.

Frequently the new worker will not have adequate work clothing. The provision of uniforms may serve the dual purpose of eliminating his anxiety that his clothing may not be socially acceptable, and of providing clothing—period! The company may offer assistance on the care of the furnished clothing.

Attractive and inexpensive eating areas should be available. Their use will give the trainee the opportunity to exchange opinions with his fellow workers of different levels. Such an experience may, in a subtle way, increase the worker's motivation and self-image.

The Final Goals

The topics discussed in this article have dealt with the determinants of the work habits of the disadvantaged worker, who lives in a different economic, cultural, and social environment from that of middle-class workers. These habits, which have been stimulated and maintained by his cultural group, have been learned in an environment of deprivation—and thus his values and social goals are different from those of his middle-class counterpart.

The hard-core worker must be offered the means to attain steady employment and a good living standard for himself and his family. A decent home will mean a more permanent family life where he can begin to make career plans for himself and his children; but all this depends upon a stable job and income.

The development of good work habits cannot be attained in a year or two. The hard-core worker's goals have been short-term ones because of the short-term jobs he has held, which have affected his hopes regarding the welfare of himself and his family. The business community must play an important part in aiding the hard-core worker to improve his status. He will be convinced of this possibility when he sees a number of others like himself getting reasonably secure jobs, a chance at promotion, and a decent place to live. If the hard-core worker is to change his negative and suspicious attitudes, then business and government must convince him that he can have better opportunities than he has historically received. Our viability and even survival as a nation will very likely depend on how we answer this challenge.

Management's Perspective in Employing the Disadvantaged

Walter Victor Rouse

THE hiring and training of persons who have been subjected to poverty and racism, causing loss of motivation, is not an easy job. To undertake such an effort without an understanding of the difficulties involved is to compound years of damage to these persons. However, if those who are responsible for training, counseling, and aiding in the development of the disadvantaged are themselves disadvantaged—in a different way—then such a training program will surely fail. A train-

WALTER VICTOR ROUSE is President, W. V. Rouse & Associates, Inc., Chicago, Illinois.

ing program of this type would be merely a showpiece and a topic for meaningless speeches by top company executives.

To hand such an important task to a training department that neither recognizes nor understands its lack of competence in this area is to reaffirm the notion that the disadvantaged really don't want to work and would prefer to remain on relief indefinitely. Minority persons will not be motivated or acclimated to the work environment when the programming fails to meet even their basic needs. Any program that involves the hiring, training, and upgrading of the disadvantaged should be well planned and properly prepared for.

Overall Criteria for the Program

Initially, decisions should be made in the following areas:

- The nature and extent of education and/or job training to be provided.
- Whether government assistance should be sought in defraying program costs.
- How much special education should be provided for supervisors and other company personnel involved in the program.
- The nature and extent of off-job assistance.
- The nature and extent of on-job support.
- The coordination of the total program.
- The number of trainees involved.
- The length of the program.
- The handling of discipline problems and how far a company should go with a trainee.
- Whether the program will be terminal or ongoing.
- What to expect from current employees as they view trainees and the program.
- What, if any, preemployment test should be used.
- How much information should be sought regarding the backgrounds of the trainees.

- Who will develop the training program. Are there people in the company who are qualified technically and who have the proper understanding?
- The commitment of top management. Does it really want a viable program?
- The involvement of current employees in tutoring or otherwise assisting trainees? (the "buddy" system). Should nearby educational institutions become involved, as well as community groups, for supportive services?
- The kind of counseling program that should be used.
- The upgrading of trainees.

In general, an effective system for employing disadvantaged persons must include:

1. An effective system of developing newly hired disadvantaged persons so that their skills will match the needs of the employer while providing job satisfaction for the individual.
2. An effective system of orienting existing plant employees to the problems inherent in absorbing disadvantaged employees. This should be in the nature of a general, continuing orientation, not something done temporarily for a specific number of disadvantaged persons.
3. An effective system of continued evaluation and upgrading of skills so that entry-level jobs do not become terminal points for the new employees.

Modern technology and current job requirements demand that applicants have certain job skills that can be matched with the needs of the employer. Today, however, proper training and skill development, though essential for mutual satisfaction of employee and employer, are only part of the effort needed. If the new employee is unable to adjust to his new and very different environment and if he is rejected, abused, and misunderstood by supervisors and fellow employees, job skills alone will be no guarantee of success.

The hard fact is that locating, training, and the placement of minority persons without serious consideration for their ability to handle the social interactions that will surely occur will lead to a defensive and uncooperative posture on the part of the new employees as well as hostility and fear on the part of management and those who will work with the new employees.

It then becomes painfully obvious that the seeking out and placement of disadvantaged persons is only the beginning of a very difficult process. Unless such an effort is carefully planned, the conditions of underemployment, rejection, and ignorance in which the new employees find themselves can lead to failure of the training project.

Persons who have suffered from poverty and racism, particularly black people, are increasingly refusing to be manipulated for the publicity of an organization. Employers must recognize the human needs and fears of both the existing workforce and the newly hired persons. Good intentions are not enough. If there is a failure to understand the need for behavioral change and to respond accordingly, the project will collapse regardless of goodwill.

A program of hiring and training must have certain specific objectives if it is to succeed:

1. Systematic training so that the new employee is able to perform as expected. The new employee must first become convinced that he can perform, and adequate training will go a long way in developing his confidence.

2. A realistic explanation from the employee about the new employee's prospects for the future. A certain growth rate should be anticipated and then revised according to the employee's progress.

3. Clear and distinct avenues of communication that are available to the employee both within the work group and to management. This may be accomplished by use of a "buddy" who is on the job daily and who may assist the new employee with his questions and

difficulties. This buddy should preferably be of the same race and have a background similar to that of the new employee. One or more persons from management who have the confidence of the new employees but who also have authority and the ear of top management should act as liaison between the buddies of the new employees and upper management.

4. A method of orienting executives and administrative, supervisory, and plant personnel that will raise the level of understanding of the program and reduce friction as the newly trained make the transition into the plant.

5. A well-defined system of evaluation of the training and of upgrading for the new employees, as well as continuous assessment of the in-house training as to its relevance and effectiveness.

Motivation of the Disadvantaged

There are several factors that might be used to influence motivation for disadvantaged persons, but before any of these are attempted, management must clearly recognize that years of denial and lack of motivation in an achievement-oriented society such as ours have placed the new employee in a difficult position. For many people, the two major sources of satisfaction are achievement and power, but for the black man and for members of other minorities, these motivational forces have had to take a back seat to simple survival.

Motivation becomes very difficult when the socially and economically disabled, who are usually minority persons, are involved. The disadvantaged employee desires the same success, material goods, and job satisfaction as other persons. What must be clearly seen, however, is that the disadvantaged employee is prevented from attaining satisfaction in his job. Once the long-employed and often-refused employee finds himself on the job, he lacks the "appreciation" that is often expected of him.

Traditional attitudes in industry. The greatest change that must occur must be within industry, which has, as a whole, traditionally and consistently rejected the economically and socially disabled person. This process starts with the recruiter or interviewer, who is often untrained in the lives and behavioral patterns of minorities; it continues with employees who have no empathy with the disadvantaged person's problems and no concern for changing his own perspective. Such ignorance, indifference, and lack of understanding exist throughout industry. Management seems to forget, when arguing productivity and profit as compared with moral duty and justice, that the human being must be fully considered. I will not attempt to convince those in management who are opposed to hiring and training the economically and socially deprived that it is good business. I will simply point out that company executives and old-line supervisors, to mention a few, argue as fundamental truth that to expect rapid movement is unrealistic because of union resistance, employee resistance, or community resistance. Change must come slowly. The argument constantly flows: "Change must be found in conscience, not through pressure."

The attitude of the disadvantaged. To the newly hired and long-deprived employee, this argument is ridiculous. Although he cannot fully articulate his view, this person is saying that arbitrary rules of conduct have developed in white society, and white industry is reacting to change because of pressure, not out of kindness or concern. This newly hired employee does not appreciate his new employer for "giving" him a job. He believes that he is entitled to it, and could, with proper motivation and communication, become a reliable and effective employee, but hardly the grovelingly grateful black man of years past. This new employee will have little compunction about doing only what is necessary and nothing more. He sees the rules of industry as foreign and the rigorous requirements of work as ridiculous and unrealistic. Because he sees the greatest rewards of his labor going to others or because there is no communication that would cause him to change his thinking, he feels little need to respect the property and rewards of others. ✓ Thus he won't mind taking what he can from those who he feels represent a group that has taken so much from him. Unless there is a well-developed training approach at all levels, the hiring of the disadvantaged will cause great unhappiness for all concerned.

Factors in interracial communication. Both blacks and whites fear that overexposure of their feelings to members of the other group is dangerous. The most effective way to communicate, however, is honestly and sincerely. Our experiences have shown us that a genuine demonstration of feelings by those attempting to communicate—whether it be in the form of questions, hostility, threats, or admiration—is most beneficial in developing sound relationships. When feelings are suppressed by whites, minority persons are likely to assume what has been historically true—that the person who is not saying what is really on his mind is prejudiced. The minority person is also fearful of overexposing himself to the white person; he is defensive because he has learned that this will protect him from both psychological and physical harm. A basically honest relationship is the most productive of all. Each party becomes secure when it is recognized that opinions are being expressed honestly and openly.

Approaches in motivating the disadvantaged. The following are some approaches used in motivating the disadvantaged:

Set specific and realistic goals. The confidence of an individual and his ability to perform are closely related to that person's ability to direct his energy toward a goal that he himself defines. An employer must act to assist in this self-actualization, not as a father directing his child, but rather as a counselor outlining possible approaches. Black people now increasingly reject what they feel is the paternalism of slavery times being reborn in new training programs. It therefore becomes most important that interviewers and personnel representatives tak to a job applicant as man or woman, not as someone less than a person. When outlining the new employee's anticipated progress, the interviewer should be absolutely honest. One thing should be paramount: The employee must, with the employer's assistance, fulfill his own inner needs. Once he sees that you the employer are sincere, it is essential that you do all you have promised, through (1) the proper types of training and upgrading that will develop the kind of confidence necessary in the trainee; and (2) the proper kind of training for all those in management, so that the new employee doesn't incur arrogance from whites that gives him the impression that he is being led and not assisted. When the individual sets his own goals, with motivation stemming from the challenge of the training and the job through such factors as achievement, responsibility, growth, and earned recognition, success for the individual and the employee will be lasting and worthwhile. As Frederick Douglass said:

> Everybody has asked the question, and they learned to ask it early of the abolitionists, "What shall we do with the negro?" I have had but one answer from the beginning. Do nothing with us! Your doing with us has already played the mischief with us. Do nothing with us! If the apples will not remain on the tree of their own strength, if they are worm-eaten at the core, if they are early ripe and disposed to fall, let them fall! I am not for tying or fastening them on the tree in any way, except by nature's plan, and if they will not stay there, let them fall. And if the negro cannot stand on his own legs, let him fall also. All I ask is, give him a chance to stand on his own legs! Let him alone! If you see him on his way to school, let him alone,—don't disturb him! If you see him going to the dinner table at a hotel, let him go! If you see him going to the ballot-box, let him alone,— don't disturb him! If you see him going into a work-shop, just let him alone,—your interference is doing him a positive injury. [*]

[*] Gilbert Osofsky, *The Burden of Race* (New York: Harper & Row, 1967), p. 152.

Stimulate the trainee's confidence. Think, talk, and act as with a man of high achievement. The new trainee has many attitudes and feelings that he will not share with others because he anticipates derision, misunderstanding, and indifference from them. It is in this area that he can be reached by properly oriented instructors, counselors, supervisors, and managers. The primary function of persons in such leadership positions is not to effect personality change in the trainee, but rather to maximize his own effectiveness where communication and a feeling of honesty are so important. As the new employee discovers that his ideas meet with understanding and respect, he will gradually become more relaxed and more able to think and act like a person who believes that he can learn and work as an effective employee. He will be able to express things that he would not have risked saying before for fear of criticism, derision, or being ignored. He will feel that he is better understood by others, grow more confident, and most likely become more energetic and ambitious. He can work much more effectively. He is more receptive to what others have to say and is more likely to make positive changes. Such changes will come from his desire to approve of his own actions. These kinds of change create lasting respect instead of hate and resentment.

Let the trainee seek his own identity. Management must be very careful in its training efforts not to influence the trainee so that he becomes as "white" as possible. If the objective of a training program is to take a black man who has been socially and economically disabled and make him a reflection of what is regarded as good by whites, then that program will fail.

A person must have pride in himself, and he will avoid experiences inconsistent with that image. For a long time, the black man has sought the approval of white society by attempting to do and say what whites wanted done and said. The black man is now seeking self-approval, and this he must do by himself; white assistance is needed, but the goal must be reached by the black man. White management can make its greatest contribution by attempting to alter the behavior of other whites. Any attempt to make new trainees extensions of themselves will fail; whether the trainees are young black militants or older persons, the degree to which they are seeking self-respect and proper treatment differs little.

When the new trainees exhibit attitudes or behavior that conflict with the personal standards of individuals within a company or an outmoded company policy, there is a tendency to reject the person. An individual with a very narrow set of values is therefore unlikely to be successful when communicating with people who have values quite different from his own. A person who is involved in the training of disadvantaged persons, or who is otherwise responsible for responding to them, must develop a broad range of values and be flexible enough to recognize that his own standards are not necessarily those of others. If this degree of understanding is realized, a person is likely to be able to communicate respect to those with whom he works.

People are usually responding to their own needs when they try to encourage people to see things the way they see them. It is particularly difficult for whites to tolerate and understand actions that are different from the way in which they believe they should act. If, however, whites are able to free themselves from the need to influence and direct blacks, they will be better able to listen with understanding, and thereby effect the greatest possible change—by changing themselves.

The Nature of the Training Programs

Training of supervisors. When a new program of training is under consideration, top management should take a careful look at its own organization to see that its supervisors and counselors receive proper training before any attempt is made to train or counsel others. This training should also include an intensive look at communications and counseling. (Some consideration should also be given to the training of *all* supervisors in the organization, since the need for such training will increase as highly trained as well as untrained minority persons are added.) It *is* true that many white managers, executives, and administrators should be categorized as "hard core," for they adamantly believe that only whites should plan and program for minority persons. They refuse to recognize that they are themselves disadvantaged—ignorant of the needs of minority persons. (In this connection, if a program of training for minority persons is considered, qualified minority persons should be involved in all phases of the preparation. This is not to say that there are not professionally qualified whites who also have the kind of understanding necessary. It *is* to say, however, that qualified black professionals should also be used, from the program's inception to its conclusion.)

Supervisors, administrators, and executives who have strong attitudes regarding minority persons are likely to be very vocal, dogmatic, and anxious to impose on others in the organization the points about which they feel most defensive, guilty, or unsure. If no effective empathy and communications training is conducted prior to the hiring of the disadvantaged, training programs are likely to become the extension of the personalities of top management. Very likely, such a program will be paternalistic and a reflection of the fears and do-goodism of top management. No matter how well-intentioned top management may be, lack of real understanding and improper preparations may be damaging to the company and its employees.

Most important in these sessions is the need to evoke comments from the participants. Once the foremen or supervisors realize that the training they are receiving will assist them in their efforts to communicate with minority persons, they will thank you for their participation.

I do not recommend the lecture approach to training, because individual differences are not recognized, and because many persons have considerable difficulty grasping verbal presentations. In addition, it does not allow genuine participation. Lectures do not reach the emotional and practical problems that supervisors bring to the meeting. Participants must be urged to contribute experiences and ideas, to ask questions, to discuss, and to work out their own ideas. Even though many, if not all, of the participants are looking for answers to expected racial problems in their departments, they are not likely to speak out unless full participation is achieved. If supervisors are not encouraged to express the doubts and fears they have about minority persons, they will not be able to make effective use of information given them. Of course, mere exposure and participation do not guarantee the behavior modifications, but the chances of change are improved.

The case study method is another form of group participation that can be effective when properly used. In this technique, a written case is presented that is similar to problems of supervisory personnel in the area of communication with minority persons. Participants are required to analyze the written material—the purpose is to develop their analytical abilities in this area. Case discussion is guided by a conference leader, who also acts as moderator.

Selection of the training personnel. When a program of training is being considered, the entire training effort should be planned long before the first trainee is introduced to the organization. Many companies have made the gigantic error of virtually drafting any black employee or their only one and making him responsible for training both the new employees and top supervisors. A black person who is untrained in communication is just as dangerous in this difficult area of training as is an untrained white person. The new persons entering the organization are sensitive men and women who have faced incompetence and ignorance all their lives; to further damage them with a half-prepared and poorly administrated program would compound the injustice. Nor is it enough to send the new trainees out for 10 or 12 weeks of remedial training and then place them on jobs that they have been "trained" to perform. Any company about to embark on the training of persons whose backgrounds are so radically foreign to the company's experience should consider only a complete program.

Features in training the disadvantaged. Programs for the

newly hired disadvantaged should include the following training features:

- Entry and orientation. The first impression is especially critical for the disadvantaged employee. He will probably have deep anxieties and suspicions about the training and work situations. Unless schedules for the first few days are planned, developed, and put into operation carefully, the achievement of the program can be seriously limited. Orientation to the training program should consist of a short period during which the trainee's apprehensions are allayed. The trainees should realize that (1) they will have the option of selecting their own goals, with guidance from trained staffs; (2) they will be free to maintain their own identities; (3) they will be allowed to say and do things that may not be completely acceptable to management; (4) they may advance toward their goals according to their demonstrated abilities; and (5) they will be encouraged to prove to themselves and to others that they are capable of accomplishment and success without "selling out." Entry and orientation should take approximately one week.
- Remediation training. This includes training in mathematics, reading, and vocabulary that will bring the trainee up to the required level of proficiency.
- Job awareness training. This involves those behavioral tools and processes needed to get along in the world of work—what is generally expected of the trainees by their employer and what their responsibilities are to the employer and to the other employees.
- Social skills training. This comprises behavior required for effective interpersonal activity in an industrial setting: the "whole man" training concept. Motivational and self-identity training should be included. There should be training discussions regarding the retention

by the trainee of his identity while working in cooperation with white and black employees in a structurally
white environment.

Placement of the trainees. When considering a program
of training for disadvantaged persons, the proper placement
of these employees during and after formal training should be
fully considered. Hiring and training is not enough. I submit
that proper counseling from professional, interested employees
acting as tutors can be very beneficial to persons in programs
of this type. This involves such things as placing trainees in
jobs that interest them. However, in making various jobs available for selection, don't include merely those requiring little
skill. Following proper motivational training, trainees will have
the confidence to try difficult assignments. Tutorial training
should allow one to two hours a day for work in such things as
the basic requirements of the job and job vocabulary. I stress
again, however, that the tutor should receive training in communication and understanding of minority persons before the
training period begins. One thing will surely happen when
proper upgrading is practiced: There will be a greater involvement on the part of a larger number of persons. The trainees will
face greater hostility from white workers whose jobs they
threaten as well as from veteran black workers who resent their
rapid progress.

Consideration of present minority employees. Management
must also be very careful when starting a program of training
and upgrading for minority persons that the long-term minority employees are not forgotten. Many have never uttered a
word of discontent. Management should not allow years of
faithful service by these people to deceive it into believing that
they are necessarily happy *now* with the company. Black people have become very adept at learning to abide with a situation. However, a look at absenteeism rates, production, and
morale might be some indication of the employees' dissatisfaction. The black revolution in this country has affected many of
these employees a lot more than management is often willing

to admit. They should be fully considered when programs of training and upgrading are planned.

Evaluation of the Program

It is important that a regular evaluation of your program be conducted. If this is properly done, it will have a positive effect on the entire training effort and act as a motivating force for the trainees. Managers must be aware of the appraisal techniques involved, understand them, and correctly use them.

One important factor here is the involvement of the appraisee in the evaluation process. The appraisal session should not be dominated by management. The appraisee should be allowed to give his own ideas. However, management should not become alarmed if the appraisee's opinions differ considerably from its own. How much participation should occur?

Discussing appraisals in general, Robert A. Sutermeister tells us the following:

> Still more valuable is the "tell and listen" approach. Here you encourage the subordinate to discuss the evaluation and express his reactions and feelings. With this method, both you and the subordinate are more likely to gain insights that will lead to a change in behavior and an improvement in the subordinate's performance. And a subordinate who is permitted to express defensive attitudes or feelings about [his manager's] opinion is less likely to resent [him].†

Many managers are able to evaluate well, but lack the ability to communicate the evaluation to a disadvantaged trainee. This evaluator might be overpatronizing, or might employ the same approach he uses with the other employees. Either course will lead to resentment on both sides. The manager will soon

† Robert A. Sutermeister, "Custom-Tailor Your Appraisals," *Supervisory Management,* Vol. 11, No. 12 (December 1966), p. 28.

feel that he can't even criticize the minority person, who will in turn consider him "just another bigot." When appraising the progress of the new trainees, the interview must be tailored to fit the situation. Bluntly telling the employee where he stands and what he is doing wrong may not be the best method. This does not mean that management should be anything but honest. However, it does mean a different approach. First emphasize that the basic purpose is to help the individual and the company improve. Talk about strengths first. To introduce the subject of weakness, first ask the individual where he thinks he could improve—criticism should be positive.

Management must be careful to appraise only performance and results. The evaluation of attitudes and personality has far too many drawbacks; it is unscientific, and it allows prejudices —conscious or unconscious—to surface. Appraisal by results allows goal setting and flexibility. If necessary, goals can be changed in the middle of the program.

By simply sitting down and discussing a man's performance with him, management will encourage his development and stimulate him to put forth a better effort. This method also allows for more contact between white managers and minority persons.

Counseling Procedures

The counseling process should start with group counseling for the trainees and proceed to individual counseling according to progress. Group counseling is based on two assumptions: (1) an individual cannot be meaningfully changed from the outside—any significant change that takes place must be self-directed, and (2) the individual will, in this process, help to create an atmosphere that will encourage self-development in the other trainees. The counselor or group leader's main function, therefore, is to get the participants actively involved and participating in developing their own potential and solving their own problems. Group counseling is necessary at the beginning because of the complete environmental change facing the trainees, with the concomitant need for group cohesion. The group may range in size from two to twenty. (I would not suggest a group much larger than twenty—the task of reaching each participant would be too difficult.) A serious attempt should be made at developing the "whole man" in the training process. Such things as identity, motivation, and individual responsibility may be included. Then, depending on individual and group progress, individual counseling should begin.

There are certain principles of counseling that should be included in both group and individual efforts. There should be a planned or structured interpersonal situation. Such a counseling session should be on the basis of an expressed or implied agreement between or among the participants. A person not desiring to take part should not be forced to do so. A counseling session, whether group or individual, should be recognized by both the counselor and the participants as something more than a casual encounter. There should be a shared expectation of some kind of event. Further, privacy should be assured, there should be no interruptions, and the purpose of the session should be fully communicated to the potential participants. The participants should also be encouraged to state what they are expecting in such a session.

After proper training, supervisors often must act as counselors. As such they must make special efforts to facilitate clear communication during the counseling sessions, be sensitive to their subordinates' feelings during the interview, and be aware of their *own* prejudices and how these might influence the counseling relationship.

Group and individual counseling should also be used for supervisors. Emphasis should be placed on developing effective two-way verbal communication. Some of the difficulties in supervisor-disadvantaged counseling relationships are as follows:

- The minority person, who is in this case also the subordinate, fears that he will be judged negatively by the supervisor.
- The subordinate feels that his job will be threatened if he expresses his true thoughts or feelings.
- The subordinate is defensive because he believes that the supervisor's role is to "put him down," and he doesn't want to provide him with that opportunity.
- The supervisor may not listen carefully, feeling that he already has the answers to the disadvantaged employee's problems.
- The supervisor may be under other pressures and thus may not take the time needed to appreciate the intensity of the trainee's feelings and to appraise his own performance.
- The subordinate may have trouble expressing himself clearly.
- The supervisor may be defensive and sensitive about the black-white relationship, and feel a need to argue with the subordinate.

There are many effective ways of removing barriers such as these. For example, the counselor might use approaches such as the following:

He says, "Let me better understand how you actually feel," instead of "Don't feel that way about it."

He tries to convey, "What do you think should be done?" as opposed to "Why don't you try this?"

He asks, "What can be done to improve communications?" rather than "Your difficulty with communication is . . ."

In conclusion, I want to emphasize that management must be particularly alert not to crush the dignity and self-respect of its disadvantaged trainees. It must be sensitive to their needs—including their need for self-identity. And it must reexamine its own preconceived notions about disadvantaged persons before it presumes to tell them what to do.

The Program:
Will It Be Viable?

John B. Kelley

Pervasive unemployment and underemployment are the most persistent and serious grievances in minority areas. They are inextricably linked to the problem of civil disorder. . . . Despite growing Federal expenditures for manpower development and training programs, and sustained general economic prosperity and increasing demands for skilled workers, about two million—white and non-white—are permanently unemployed. About 10 million are underemployed, of whom six and a half million work full time for wages below the poverty line.*

JOHN B. KELLEY is President, Avco Economic Systems Corporation, Washington, D.C.
* *The National Report of the Advisory Commission on Civil Disorders* (New York: Bantam Books, 1968), pp. 413–14.

Once your company decides to hire the hard-core unemployed, it has taken a significant step in helping to make the "American dream" a reality for all our citizens. The decision is your company's response to the urgent plea of the disadvantaged. You cannot realistically expect to solve all the socio-economic ills of our nation, but you can do something about upgrading the quality of life in your own community.

Your initial decision is only the start of what can be a long and sometimes disheartening journey. Once the decision to involve one's company is made, the reality of having to deliver on one's promises can become a heavy burden. On the other hand, the intelligent employment of the hard-core unemployed can become one of the most satisfying, exciting, and rewarding experiences your firm can enjoy.

For most people, the hard-core unemployed represent the black Americans living in our urban centers. To a large extent this is true; however, it depends on where your operations are located. In many cities and rural areas the disadvantaged are black. In other areas they are Indians, Puerto Ricans, Mexican Americans, Anglo-Saxons, or Orientals. Numerically, most disadvantaged people are poor whites from a wide ethnic background. In short, the disadvantaged represent a significant cross section of America. They are people on welfare, with prison records, with obsolete or nonexistent skills, without a basic education, and often without hope for the future. Although they are often accused of exploiting our society through criminal acts and cheating, they often represent the most exploited group of people in our nation. Disadvantaged people find many doors leading to opportunity closed to them because of their color or their national or religious background. They often have to pay more for housing, food, clothing, financing, and other necessities. They are often the products of an inferior educational system, which serves to perpetuate their poverty. A small percentage of the hard-core unemployed strike out in violence to call attention to their despair.

Management's Need for Education

The previous discussion is presented as a background to the challenges involved in hiring and training the disadvantaged. It should indicate that after the decision to hire has been made, top managers, especially those who will be responsible for the firm's training program, must educate themselves regarding the socioeconomic, cultural, and psychological aspects of the people they will be employing. They should also be familiar with the experiences of other companies in this area.

The second stage is research. You will have to find out just who are the hard-core unemployed in your community; how many there are; where they are located; what the problems are that make them disadvantaged; and what your community has or has not done to help them. It would be worthwhile for you to go into their neighborhoods to talk with their leaders and spokesmen; to experience confrontations with militants; and generally to become *aware* of the often-forgotten world in which they live. The important thing is to ask intelligent, timely questions, and to *listen.* Your approach will be relevant and will more likely be interpreted as genuine if you are informed.

The advantages of the self-education and research stages are as follows:

■ You have a better understanding of the dimensions of the poverty problem and of the characteristics of the disadvantaged.

■ You have a better understanding of your own feelings, attitudes, and prejudices toward the hard core.

■ You know what your community, state, and federal governments are doing about the problem, their successes, failures, and potential for the future.

■ You know what other companies have done, and you can learn from their experiences.

■ You know what government and private services are available to help you. You may also find that there are various sources of funds available to help ease your burden and to help you succeed with your program.

■ You know where to recruit the disadvantaged.

■ You have a better understanding of how the disadvantaged live, think, consider the future, and react.

■ You also find out if you really want to go ahead with your proposed program for hiring the hard core. The self-education and research stages allow you to rethink your intended involvement. A "no-go" decision would be based on knowledge, not lack of it. A "go" decision would, on the other hand, be based on analysis instead of unrealistic optimism.

■ You have the opportunity to find out how your employees feel about working with the hard core. This foreknowledge would help to shape the attitudes of your workers. A proposed program to hire and train the disadvantaged could be sold to present workers not as a threat to job security, but as good business and good sense for the community.

■ Finally, the self-education and research stages are unique opportunities to upgrade and make relevant traditional personnel policies and practices in order to provide those individuals involved in the program—management, present employees, union representatives, and the disadvantaged—with opportunities for individual growth.

The knowledge gained from the first, exploratory phase forms the basis from which a plan to hire and train the hard core can be developed. It is difficult for an outsider to tell you what kind of plan you should make, what goes into it, and how best to implement it. However, I can present several key considerations that may help to give your plan a greater sense of reality:

■ Consider the optimum number of hard-core unemployed workers you can take on initially, in proportion to the number of those you require from the ranks of the skilled. Will this effort require lowering the quota of skilled new employees in preference to hiring the disadvantaged? How many hard-core unemployed can you afford to hire, train, and employ in addition to your present workforce?

■ Consider whether such a program will be short-term or continuous. Will it provide for hiring just one group of hard-core unemployed and call the job done, or will it be standing policy to hire the disadvantaged in accordance with the expanding personnel requirements of the business?

■ Consider how far you want to stretch existing personnel policies (such as lateness, misconduct, probationary periods, personal appearance, and so forth) to accommodate the disadvantaged worker.

■ Consider what approach you will use for on-the-job training.

■ Consider your approach to counseling the disadvantaged worker regarding his personal and job-oriented problems.

■ Consider how outside training and support services can help both the worker and the company.

■ Consider how to encourage the disadvantaged worker to advance in skill levels.

■ Consider how your more liberal practices with the disadvantaged will affect the morale and productivity of your present employees.

■ Consider how much extra time and effort will be required to transform a disadvantaged individual into a skilled and productive worker.

■ Consider the best way of providing your disadvantaged workers with supplementary education, such as the opportunity to improve their reading, writing, and mathematical skills.

■ Consider how you will deal with conflict situations between or among workers, and between management and workers.

■ Consider how the unions can assist in your program.

These are but a sampling of the many key considerations that must go into any plan involving the disadvantaged worker. Initially, several alternative plans should be developed and evaluated. Again, the self-education and research stages will prove to be most valuable in the formulation of a practical plan. After the plan has been selected, it must be flexible enough to evolve into a more sophisticated approach as the program itself progresses. It is understandable that since hiring the disadvantaged is complex sociologically, a rigid approach may be developed more because of uncertainty than because of indifference. Since a rigid approach can be self-defeating, extreme care must be taken to make the plan open to change. It may not be the best possible plan at first, but if it is flexible, it has a good chance of succeeding.

The Value of the Program

When you do have a plan, it will take a great deal of patience, intelligence, goodwill, and creativity to make it work. The question continues to be, "Is it worth it?" If your plan is sound and sufficiently flexible, and if the program is enthusiastically implemented and supported, from top management through the ranks to the trainees themselves, then you have a good chance of ending up with a new group of regular employees, who may turn out to be more highly motivated than your regular workforce. Your commitment to this kind of program will strengthen your image as a responsible and creative community leader. Your involvement may even result in increased business. Today's trend, both nationally and locally, is toward increased private enterprise involvement in helping to solve our socioeconomic problems.

Whether they live in ghettos, reservations, or rural areas, most disadvantaged persons are honest men and women who would rather work than be idle. Short periods of idleness for the busy, productive, happy man are the means by which he builds up his energies and spirit so that he can continue to be useful. Long-term unemployment or underemployment for the disadvantaged person results in a breakdown of spirit and of the will to make an effort. Thus it is not surprising that when a company executive offers jobs to the hard-core unemployed, he is sometimes met with indifference or hostility.

No one expects a businessman also to be a psychologist; but the question remains: How can the businessman motivate the hard-core unemployed to work for him? Let me offer the following possible solution to this complex question. First of all, nobody wants to be a loser. Yet for many of the disadvantaged, constant failure—in schools, jobs, and personal life—has been the norm in their lives. As one black ghetto dweller expressed it, "You learn to live with the fact that you are a loser . . . anything else would seem like some nice dream that never could come true." With this reality in mind, if a company could approach the "unemployables" on the basis that "we want you to succeed—you can succeed with us because we are successful ourselves and we will help to make you a success," then there is a good chance that the man will respond positively. You might put it this way: "Here's a chance to really make it . . . a chance for a piece of the action." Success is contagious.

Avco Economic Systems Corporation has a continuing program to hire and train disadvantaged persons. Some of our experiences might be relevant for the small- or medium-size company. The May 6, 1968, issue of *Newsweek* magazine described one of our hard-core unemployed hiring projects in this manner:

The scene was, to say the least, a bit bizarre. There in a former coal dump in the black ghetto of Roxbury [a section of Boston, Massachusetts] was James R. Kerr, the President of Avco Corporation, wielding a ceremonial bronze shovel. Beside him, resplendent in a leopard-skin poncho and Black Muslim amulet, was one of Avco's newest employees, Ted Wheaton—and it was Wheaton who introduced the boss when the time came for him to speak.

Kerr was in Roxbury . . . to break ground for what is probably the most ambitious effort by U.S. industry so far to bring plants into the ghetto and provide jobs for ghetto dwellers. Avco . . . [has put up] a brand-new $1.2 million plant in the heart of Roxbury, filled it with $700,000 worth of new machinery and staffed it with 250 local Negroes and Puerto Ricans. Within three years the plant is to handle all of Avco's corporate printing work—at present, a $3 million annual item—and branch into contract work for other firms.

Avco started with one government contract: $1.1 million from the Labor Department, to be matched by the company for recruiting and training of ghetto workers. Robert Earle, a 50-year-old administrative man who had been with the company for eleven years, was told to take over the program and start a year-long hiring and training program for 250 people—15 percent of them ex-convicts, 10 percent mothers on welfare, 25 percent hard-core unemployed and 50 percent employed only part time or at marginal jobs.

Earle's . . . team of Avco executives start the new workers with a month of what amounts to therapy for cultural shock: motivational training, remedial reading and writing, English, shop, math, and "minority history"—a course in race relations and Negro history. As in most ghetto projects absenteeism is a problem; but [the] personnel manager . . . personally knocks on a trainee's door if he hasn't shown up for more than one day. Wages start at $80 a week, with a maximum of $193. Most important, the trainees are guaranteed a "career ladder" in the printing trades.

This Avco experience indicates that when you give a person an opportunity, the chances are better than even that he will do everything he can to succeed. All the disadvantaged person wants is what most Americans have—a chance to acquire the "good life" for himself and his family, honestly and with dignity.

Your Approach to the Program

Outside assistance. Since funding of and assistance for your program may be essential to its success, the following sources of help should be explored:

- The National Alliance of Businessmen (NAB), under JOBS, a program coordinated with federal programs, will provide information on federal and private community resources for training, recruiting, and other services.
- The Manpower Administration of the United States Department of Labor is responsible for most federal programs involving recruitment, training, and placement. You should contact a regional office of the Administration for information on funding and technical assistance. The Manpower Administration conducts such programs as apprenticeship training, on-the-job training, Neighborhood Youth Corps, Work Incentive Program, and Concentrated Employment Program.
- Other resources of recruitment and training include: the Community Action Program, under the Office of Economic Opportunity; the Job Corps Program, now under the Department of Labor; and the Social and Rehabilitation Services, under the Department of Health, Education, and Welfare.

More and more companies from the private sector are also getting into the business of training on a contract basis. Avco Economic Systems Corporation is one of these. The services of such companies should be considered because of their experience with and understanding of the problem of training the disadvantaged worker. Recruitment and training assistance can also be obtained from such organizations as the Opportunities Industrialization Center (OIC), the National Association for the Advancement of Colored People (NAACP), and the Urban League. State and commercial employment agencies, welfare agencies, church and civic groups, social and fraternal organizations, and ethnic and militant groups can be considered as good recruitment sources.

The training managers. The steps presented thus far may become meaningless unless the people operating your program are capable of making it work. The qualities of leadership for running a program for employing and training the hard-core unemployed are not unlike those for any other cooperative effort. Such qualities should include:

- Courage to make difficult decisions in often highly emotion-charged situations.

- Compassion to see life from the other man's point of view, and reluctance to impose a middle-class value system on people who have reason to distrust such a system.

- Honesty to "tell it like it is," without cover-ups or phony approaches. Honest, reasonable candor will win more respect for you than will a patronizing or abrasive attitude.

- Patience in understanding that the process of transforming the disadvantaged into productive and loyal workers may be slow and often discouraging.

- Competence in performing on the job, in a position of leadership, as a mediator in disputes, and as a teacher.

- Justice, dispensed fairly and promptly. Disadvantaged people are used to getting the short end of justice.

- Objectivity, in seeing the true reality of each situation.

- Sincerity and interest in a man's progress, difficulties, and problems. It means a lot to know that your boss wants you to succeed.

- Optimism that in the long run, if your plan, leadership, and attitudes are right, you will see the majority of your disadvantaged employees develop into productive workers.

This list is far from complete, but it presents some of the criteria that must be considered when selecting the kind of people who will direct the program and act as liaison between management and the new employees.

These leaders must have the complete support of top management. In turn, top management should make it clear to middle-level managers and to first-line supervisory personnel that its decision to employ and train the disadvantaged is a definite commitment and must be supported. Managers and supervisory personnel must, in turn, convey and enforce this order to their respective staffs and workforces. The degree of worker acceptance will depend on how effectively this is done. If possible, key supervisors should go through a "sensitizing" or educational process to help them understand the difficult circumstances affecting the disadvantaged worker. Such sensitivity training of corporate personnel is recognized as important for firms taking advantage of Department of Labor funds for training.

Some may complain that the new employees will receive preferential treatment. It is important that the current employees be informed why this special treatment must be provided initially, and that once the trainee becomes a regular employee, he will be treated no differently from the rest. The disadvantaged worker prefers to be regarded in the same way as the other employees, but the initial phase of employment is probably more difficult for him than for the others.

Criteria for the training personnel. The teachers you hire must be creative and want to work with your trainees. If your company is large enough and the program is expected to continue for a few years, it might be worthwhile to have an "in-house" staff formed into a special education department whose services are available to all employees. It must be noted that education is America's primary industry and that the inventory of materials, techniques, and experts it annually generates should be utilized in improving and updating your training programs. Also, the entire field of vocational skills training has progressed so rapidly that it can almost be thought of as a science in itself. Your training people should continually be abreast of the latest techniques.

Hiring criteria. Part of the traditional approach to hiring is based on what a person has accomplished in the past. Men with "clean" records are preferred to those with a history of infractions against the law. This standard is not relevant when hiring the disadvantaged. Although many will come to you with clean records, some may be former convicts, narcotics addicts, or alcoholics, or have serious financial problems. Since you have made a commitment to hire the disadvantaged, you must be flexible with regard to an individual's past record.

Early-training techniques. After the person has been hired, the company should immediately cease to refer to him as "hard core" or as "disadvantaged." He in fact becomes a trainee. The emphasis should be on making him feel as comfortable as possible in his new job environment and lessening the image that he is somehow different from the other workers.

It is common personnel practice to employ testing to determine the work aptitudes and potentials of individuals. The General Aptitude Test Battery has been used successfully to discover the aptitudes of disadvantaged workers. The GATB approach consists of tests to determine the following aptitudes: general learning ability, verbal aptitude, numerical aptitude, spatial aptitude, form perception, clerical perception, motor coordination, finger dexterity, and manual dexterity.

This GATB approach can be purchased for use within the company. However, many state departments of employment will administer and interpret the test results for you. The latter approach will be less costly to your firm, and the interpretation of the results will tend to be more valid.

Another aptitude test to consider is the Kuder Preference Vocational Test. It can be used as an objective basis for evaluation of an individual's aptitude in broad vocational areas.

The areas of orientation, on-the-job training, remedial education, and counseling should form the substance of your training program. They are the means by which you help the individual transform himself into a productive and loyal worker.

The orientation period should last as long as necessary to acquaint the trainee with the program; what is expected of him during and after the program; and how he can benefit from his participation in a team effort. The orientation may last from one to two weeks. It may be necessary to provide a course which would include such things as personal appearance, balancing one's checkbook, punching a time clock, and an explanation of the workings of the business world in general and your company in particular.

Remedial education should be job-related. A large part of remedial education is centered in the areas of reading and communication skills; however, this emphasis tends to be relative, depending on the needs of a particular company. Therefore, some firms may want to concentrate on mathematics and engineering-oriented subjects. At Avco our experience has shown that a pupil-teacher ratio of seven to one works well in remedial education.

The subject matter taught in remedial education should tie in with or have relevance to the type of work the trainee will be doing. In addition, it should be something he can use to improve the quality of his life outside the business.

On-the-job training (OJT). This is a training technique familiar to most businesses. Most people learn and become proficient in their job by actually doing it. OJT should form the substance of your program with the formerly disadvantaged worker. Avco's Roxbury plant uses the job coach system in the OJT stage, which runs for approximately 21 weeks. The individual's progress is discussed and evaluated with him by his coach, counselor, and supervisor in such a way that the trainee learns from his mistakes. Analysis of his strengths is presented to him in a way that serves to build and reinforce a strong sense of pride in himself and his accomplishments.

The probationary period. At this point, one may inquire about the three- to six-month probationary period that most companies use with new employees. Early in the program, you should inform your trainees about the company's policy in this regard. State this simply and directly, and emphasize that the policy is applicable to *all* new workers. You may have to extend the probationary period in certain exceptional cases, but you must be firm in enforcing dismissal when there is no other recourse.

The counseling program. An effective counseling program can contribute greatly to making your efforts with the disadvantaged worker a success. Group and individual counseling are both being used by many companies. Group counseling involves several trainees and counselors who discuss each other's problems, grievances, and successes. Through this method the individual trainee is able to achieve clearer insight into his own situation and that of others. Equally important, he finds out that his problems are not unique. This constructive interaction with his peers is a valuable learning process, which can form the basis for developing a sense of teamwork with and trust in his co-workers.

Individual counseling is a one-man-to-one-man (counselor and trainee) approach. Often the counselor must play many roles, such as friend, critic, and father confessor. He can help the trainee in many different ways. For example:

- He establishes rapport based on trust and confidence.
- He keeps in close touch with the trainee in order to discuss and solve problems on the job. Leaving the man to settle affairs on his own can result in lost man-hours and even the failure of the man in the job.
- He conveys the man's frustrations and grievances to management before they erupt, with possibly serious consequences to the program or even to the business itself.
- He is a source of referral to organizations such as hospitals, welfare and subsistence agencies, legal aid groups, and child care agencies, which the disadvantaged may continue to require for some time. Sometimes requests for such information are not made for the worker himself but for relatives and friends who need help and look to the worker for advice.
- He can provide trainees with advanced educational materials and information about how and where a trainee can take advantage of extension courses, higher education, and scholarships.

The counselor and his staff must be carefully selected. Although it is desirable to have an experienced professional as counselor, you may find that a person less experienced and educated can be utilized if he has an interest in and aptitude for such a position, and if he has the quality of being able to motivate people to renew their efforts to achieve excellence in their activities.

Most programs will require one full-time counselor for each

eight-hour shift. Experience with one of our programs in employing the disadvantaged showed that after we provided counseling on a 24-hour basis, the monthly loss of man-hours was cut from approximately 17.9 percent to about 5.2 percent. To say that counseling is essential is an understatement. One of the goals of the counseling process is to help the individual believe in himself enough so that he will take increasingly more responsibility in determining his own progress.

Winning your trainees' loyalty. Every businessman wants loyal employees, and almost every workingman would like to feel proud of his job and of where he works. The feeling that he is contributing to making his team a winner gives a man a strong sense of identity with his company. We have already talked about some of the things that a company can do to help a man feel like a winner—but there are more. First of all, fringe benefits like a retirement plan, a medical plan, and two weeks' vacation do not impress the disadvantaged worker as much as one might think. He has been familiar with this kind of security before—in the form of welfare and charity. And he knows where to go for more of the same, should he leave your employ. For many people, two weeks' vacation is a most welcome benefit. To the man with a past history of forced idleness, two weeks' vacation can represent going back to a state of life from which he has taken great pains to escape. You should be in a position to let the man sell back to you a portion of his vacation time so that he can stay on the job. If possible, give him the choice of continuing to work or taking a vacation. Another way to get the man involved with the company is through a recreation program. This means a corporate bowling, baseball, basketball, or other sports team. Company parties, banquets, picnics, and so forth, help to make the man feel more a part of the corporate family. Some companies organize trips for their employees to sports events, musical programs, movies and plays, to large cities, and even sponsor international travel. The whole idea is that the company represents much more to the man than just an exchange of hours for dollars.

Another factor that builds employee loyalty is the interest

the company takes in the man's community. The interest can be expressed by top management knowing and becoming friendly with the power structure of a ghetto: businessmen, politicians, clerics, cultural leaders, militants, and the people themselves. Executives can seek to participate in ghetto community committees, social events, cultural affairs, and anything else that gives exposure and expresses sincere, honest interest. It would be worthwhile for officials to visit the homes of their employees and get to know their families. An executive's time is at a premium, of course, but to be effective he must constantly recharge his understanding of the world in which he operates. Such involvement as described above can be an excellent way for you to secure new perspectives and fresh vision.

Your program for employing the hard core will affect your traditional personnel policies. If the matter is approached intelligently, these changes can be regarded as constructive, benefiting all employees, and not as a disruptive influence leading to resentment and conflict. If your approach is sound, the large majority of your formerly disadvantaged trainees will cooperate fully with your program and will enter the ranks of your regular employees. Even with an outstanding plan, expect a certain amount of turnover, conflict situations, and discouragement. Patience, sensitivity, vision, and a high sense of the reality of your situation will contribute greatly to making your program a success.

As an introduction to this article I used a quote from the study conducted by the Commission on Civil Disorders. I would like to close with a statement by Mitchell I. Ginsberg, New York City Human Resources Administrator, before the Commission: "Our present system of public welfare is designed to save money instead of people, and tragically ends up doing neither."†

It is conceivable that by hiring the disadvantaged, business can save both people and money.

† *Ibid.*, p. 457.

The Program:
A Two-Way Street

Adolph Holmes

W_E are entering a period in personnel administration that still contains unspoken attitudes, preconceived notions, and distorted myths nurtured by both unemployed, disadvantaged workers and their potential employers. This need not be a cause for despair; clearly, a tremendous potential for change exists in the next few years. For the most part, the dearth of research literature available in this area is analogous to the existence of the visible structural remnants of American slavery—that is to say, it is virtually nonexistent. We are entering, therefore, a new era, but one that still contains unspoken silent attitudes, preconceived notions, and generalized myths on the part of both the unemployed black worker and firms managed by

ADOLPH HOLMES is Associate Program Director, National Urban League, Inc., New York.

whites. Management can expect to be deluged by a diversity of new ideas in the areas of hiring and training. I submit, however, that a new, expanded awareness of human relationships on the part of management, combined with a greater use of common sense and a perception of *all* individuals as persons, will be of primary significance. Generally speaking, we can expect to witness the continued erosion of the caste system with which this nation has been burdened for more than 350 years, the legal structure of which has only begun to be shattered in the last six years. The basis of this system, of course, has been color, which has been deeply imbedded in the marrow of every American institution and effectively transmitted to each of us.

Careful introspection should precede any technical considerations for the manager contemplating hiring the hard-core disadvantaged. Such self-examination is prerequisite to determining what he can expect such a program to yield for his firm.

A firm's stated expectations are usually high at the beginning of a training program, and its enthusiasm for the program will be transmitted to the training staff and the trainees. However, they too have been conditioned to anticipate inadequate support and "business as usual." Consider today's present emphasis on training and equal employment compared with its almost complete absence at the beginning of the 1960s. The introduction to a small business textbook at that time, by an Ivy League academician, opened with the following:

"Among the best loved folk heroes of America—the homespun country editor, the faithful old darky, the village schoolmaster, surely the self-made businessman has a place."

To what extent is such an absurd contradiction in terms prevalent today? Not long ago, the vice-president for personnel of one of the world's largest insurance companies, which employs thousands of women, boastfully mentioned that his company "has been hiring 'colored girls' since 1954." My first impression was of the raw courage these young ladies had to demonstrate in making this pioneering venture into such a demanding situation, coupled with the tragedy of their mothers', and particularly of their fathers' exclusion—for they had had no opportunity whatsoever to work in such a setting. I did not express these thoughts, because the officer's next words were "and they even eat with us in the cafeteria." One immediately questions how effective policy implementation can be at the line level when the highest echelons of corporate administration, the responsible sources, express these attitudes about fellow adult Americans.

The task of securing employment is frequently an immensely trying experience for the disadvantaged applicant—a fact not often perceived by personnel. I recently spoke with an officer of a large corporation concerning a major effort by his firm to recruit production workers for its assembly line. A total of 250 applicants came from various poverty centers. However, only 18 people were hired. In effect, this officer recruited 250 "bodies" without informing the poverty center directors that the company's regular preemployment tests would be given. The applicants' belief that they were once again "screened out" would now be reinforced. The technique of prescreening at the poverty centers had been overlooked by both the employer and the centers' directors. Although understandably disappointed, the officer's comment was, "And how many will stay?"

It is obvious that today's personnel administrator has his work cut out for him, particularly if he is with a moderate-size or small company and thus is responsible for more than one major function.

What I want to emphasize is the need to continually view both sides of the coin, and to remember that your ideas of past, present, and future, in terms of both personal experience and corporate personnel activities, are qualitatively different from the disadvantaged worker's perceptions of and experiences with these same concepts. In addition, the disadvantaged worker's self-image has also been different from your own in terms of expectation and fulfillment. You are literally beginning to work with individuals from whom you have been culturally disassociated by fiat and custom.

Preliminary Considerations

Perhaps the first question is, "Why should my firm get involved?" There is domestic disorder in our nation that is putting formidable pressure on business. A host of committees and organizations have been set up, and ambitious statements have been made, outlining extensive programs. The following is typical of the phrasing used for such programs:

> "Detroit tries to hear it like it is; business trying to aid and defuse the ghetto . . ."

> "Should business tackle society's problems?"

> "Private enterprise's response to the huge burdens abdicated by the public sector raises an issue the voters must decide."

> "To prevent a chain of super-Watts, business takes greater initiative."

> "What does the businessman owe society?"

> "Private WPA-business should be aware of creating make-work jobs . . ."

I submit that such approaches as these are impersonal, distant, triangling, and indecisive to those whose everyday business involves personal communication with employees.

Your firm may or may not encounter other kinds of pressure —for example, that exerted by third parties interested in or demanding to know precisely what you are doing in your hiring and training operations. These pressures are not new, of course. Beginning in the 1930s, a cohesive administrative approach developed in personnel management. Employment techniques had been refined to create a comprehensive approach toward staffing problems at all levels. The combined forces that shaped this system were unionism and wartime regulations, as well as increasing interest on the part of management in research progress in the social sciences. Today, a prime contractor or subcontractor can expect periodic visits from a Defense Department compliance officer. If employees number 100 or more, a firm must submit form EEOC-1, which provides Washington with a male/female breakdown of black, Spanish-surname, and other workers in a variety of occupational classifications.

Obviously, the moderate-size company has an interest in portraying a positive corporate image to the public. The chances are that a firm of this size will not be the target of a selective buying campaign, such as Rev. Jesse Jackson's "Operation Breadbasket," nor that militants and radicals will insist on participating with its present black employees in revising existing hiring and upgrading practices.

In any event, once top management has decided to undertake a program for the recruitment, screening, employment, training, and perhaps upgrading of the disadvantaged, certain follow-up procedures will be necessary. Basic vocational skills must be taught, and remedial classes conducted, if needed. Evaluation, follow-up, and performance criteria must be established to determine the effectiveness of these programs. To what end? The number of hard-core unemployed put on the payroll will, to a certain extent, raise the per capita or family income level in the disadvantaged community in a given city; this in turn will have the effect of an increased economic multiplier within that community. But the specific and immediate concern of management should be to demonstrate a visible and energetic effort that will portray the company as interested in utilizing the abilities and productive capacities of disadvantaged trainees. If there is no prospect for the trainees to assume responsible, productive positions, they will know it and act accordingly—either by leaving the program or by not taking the job seriously. A firm obviously does not want this program contamination to occur, but this can occur, quite easily, when the new group starts "rapping" at break time, during lunch, or after work. Such peer group perceptions are most difficult to reshape.

A firm is aware of its turnover rate on various job lines and categories on the basis of annual statistics, and of those for the first 30 or 90 days of employment. These statistics can be compared with those for the training program. A firm's emphasis on stable employment will be perceived by the trainee as interest in him as a person rather than as concern solely with the product, efficiency, and production schedules.

I am often amazed at first-line supervisors' referral to "whozis" or "whatsisname on machine No. 18." Such lack of personal recognition of employees is even more likely to occur with the average supervisor who is working with minority group persons for the first time. You must stress the need for recognition as one aspect of the supervisor-employee interrelationship. The first-line supervisor is the key individual in the success or failure of such a venture at the operational level. Let us consider this man in greater detail.

The first-line supervisor. This person usually considers himself a man who has, through sheer effort, succeeded by pulling himself up by his own bootstraps. Often his attitude is, "If *I* made it on my own, why can't *they?*" He is usually not aware that he has been catapulted along as part of the economic boom that followed World War II. Nor is he usually aware that the manpower shortage created by the war, coupled with the relatively low birthrate of the 1930s, was also a factor contributing to his successful rise. In general, such men are overly concerned with their status as supervisors; they tend to focus on how disadvantaged persons relate to them, rather than how they relate to the disadvantaged. Clearly, adjustment is required in such instances in order to achieve a more balanced relationship between supervisor and trainee. Initially, this can be accomplished in sensitivity sessions conducted by supportive services specialists called in to deal with situations such as this.

Advantages of smaller companies. In the moderate- or small-to-moderate-size firm, our experience leads us to believe that there are certain inherent advantages in *lack of* size. Obviously, it is more expensive to take an experienced supervisor —a valued asset to the firm—away from his job for a special project of this nature. Another cost arises from the difficulty of adhering to a rigid schedule because of the everyday demands of a smaller operation. But there are offsetting compensations. A trainee often experiences a more personalized kind of training. He receives more attention, although the shop is "busier," and he is exposed to a greater variety of experience in a shorter period of time. A greater informality is often present, which means that training sessions will not consist of mechanical, cut-and-dried procedures. Often a "buddy system" seems to evolve spontaneously in this atmosphere. Even the absence of an elaborate fringe-benefits package is often counterbalanced by a higher hourly wage rate.

Factors in Recruitment

Recruitment criteria. How should recruitment begin? If your firm submits a proposal to the Department of Labor for funding under the National Alliance of Businessmen's MA-6 program, trainees can be referred from a local State Employment Service (SES) office, the local Concentrated Employment Program (CEP) office, or a Manpower Multi-Service Center, or be recruited by your staff or recommended by your employees. In any event, final selection is always yours. The characteristics of a hard-core disadvantaged person must be: family income below the poverty level as determined by standards established by the Social Security Administration; unemployed or underemployed; and also either (1) a school dropout, (2) under 21 or over 45 years of age, (3) physically or mentally handicapped, or (4) subject to special obstacles (for example, a member of a minority group).

Transportation problems. Recruitment also presents particular obstacles if a business is located in a suburban area. There will be transportation difficulties, since most of the trainees will not have a car, and many will be without a driver's license. There is a high probability that such individuals will live far from the job site, because of restrictive housing patterns and the cost of financing housing, when it has been available. Even if the company is now located within an urban area, it may have plans to relocate. The U.S. Department of Transportation has been conducting pilot projects to test the effectiveness of supplemental bus programs to provide peak-hour transportation from central city areas to suburban industrial sites and to accommodate some second- and third-shift schedules; such service has generally been unavailable.

Cooperation of unions. Since a moderate-size firm doesn't carry the same weight as a larger corporation, another worry involves securing the cooperation of the employees' local, if you have a union shop. The cooperation of the local union is essential, even if this is not specified in the collective bargaining agreement, particularly where training for upgrading will occur. The principle of seniority—time in grade—must be acknowledged for union cooperation in this area. Under any contract funded by the Labor Department, the union will specify that the training plan's wages, benefits, conditions of work, and so forth, in no way violate the bargaining agreement (occasionally, a letter of intent from management specifying this will suffice). Apprenticeable positions cannot be part of an NAB effort, since the certification, recruitment, selection, and other conditions of indenture are under the egis of the particular union and the Labor Department's Bureau of Apprenticeship and Training. On the national level, the AFL-CIO has wholeheartedly endorsed the training of the disadvantaged worker, and, in fact, has established the Human Resources Development Institute, which is a counterpart of NAB; it has contracted through the Labor Department to work with key metropolitan union bodies and officers and with local management groups for more effective upgrading of underemployed workers through part-time training. In addition, its staff interprets various manpower programs to local union officials and business agents.

The attitude of the disadvantaged. What does the disadvantaged individual perceive of the world of work in general and of your firm in particular? He sees the whole as an infinite series of obstacles that the advantaged person views as incentives. The disadvantaged person knows that automation continues to remove "his" job, the job of the unskilled or semi-skilled worker. He sees the superhighway system as providing greater mobility and convenience, but for others; for him it has merely compounded the resident density of his neighborhood. Indeed, within metropolitan areas these roads have usurped the railroad's idiom of "the other side of the tracks."

Skepticism will be rampant among these new trainees during many of your orientation sessions, and for excellent reasons. If you overly stress advancement possibilities, remember first the trainee's comprehension of basic organization. He knows vaguely of a firm's pyramid of line and staff, which permits a degree of getting ahead, of course, but within restricted, reasonable limitations. He cannot pursue most career lines because of his limited experience, education, or personal contacts. Many of his friends have abilities, talents, and qualifications, but they're not making it either. And it isn't necessary for him to read the findings of a recent EEOC survey of the corporate headquarters of 100 major U.S. firms to know that there are very few administrative and clerical employees from minority groups. Contrast this with the ease with which English-speaking white aliens are actively recruited for such positions. A company's front-office image can readily give the lie to its advancement selling point.

Management will insist that the job it is offering is a steady one, and it will stress other, more tangible benefits. However, the wage rate may not equal the $3 per hour that the trainee has earned as a day laborer, where there were no deductions of any sort—just cash-in-hand at the end of the day. Contrast this with deductions for federal and state withholding taxes, health insurance, unemployment insurance, FICA, and retirement, with cash postponed for at least one week. The trainee has not experienced most of these factors.

Review for the moment the prime job satisfaction factors; traditionally there are seven: wages; physical job conditions; independence—a degree of freedom from immediate supervision; job interest; fair treatment by management; good relationships with co-workers; and steadiness of employment. The wage package has been mentioned as one example where differences in perception exist. Many other examples can be given in this area, as well as for the other six job satisfaction factors. However, it is necessary that constructive interrelationships be developed and nurtured with the trainees from this initially barren common ground.

Criteria for testing. I submit that personnel administration will eagerly accept this challenge as it has historically coped with other demands. During the "scientific management" phase of personnel administration, the overemphasis on work methods, time studies, and job assignments was modified in order not to neglect the human aspects of work. Similarly, the last few years have seen a modification in the degree of reliance on elaborate tests and scientific "systems" of dealing with applicants. Undoubtedly, part of this reconsideration had to do with pressure brought to bear by poverty programs and civil rights enactments as well as genuine doubt as to the reliability and validity of such tests. Careful review of a test manual and, for example, *Boros Mental Measurements Yearbook* will show ample need for more precise sampling of populations and item selection in the development of tests. A cutback in the amount of testing is reported, but this may be a result of the tremendous clerical shortage. In situations where testing has been waived, advancement later on has been severely limited.

The job interview. The recruitment staff's expertise in the interview situation must be given the highest priority. The degree of reliance now given to pencil-and-paper testing does not apply with the hard core. The traditional rule-of-thumb for success potential—an applicant's job history of stable and ordered work experience—cannot be applied. What, then, should be discussed in a job interview?

The interviewer should attempt to elicit from the applicant a description of his general goals, what skills he hopes to acquire, and what these could mean to his life. In other words, the degree to which an applicant can verbalize his aspirations is a prime indicator of his potential vocational maturity. It might be difficult for many interviewers to elicit this response, because much professional training is oriented toward indirect methods of counseling. An additional problem is involved when English is not the applicant's first language.

The Training Period

The value of training. Comments such as "I heard about the job from a friend" or "What kind of jobs have you got?" are sure indications of vocational vagueness. Even so, this vagueness need not be a reason for rejection. Many trainees will acquire a sense of the value of training *after* placement in a training situation. This becomes evident when a trainee quits upon discovering that his new job is not a *learning* training experience. The trainee—if he is a school dropout or even high school graduate, but semiliterate—will have to be taught *how* to learn. Therefore, provision should be made for classes in basic vocational English. Such rudimentary language acquisition is necessary, because some trainees want to succeed very badly but cannot understand what is being taught. It appears that most industry-sponsored language training is a surface, brush-up program of vocational English. At a particular plant, where previous training programs have stressed safety procedures exclusively, a more individualized training approach is being taken. An example is the posting of bilingual signs in the plant.

The training personnel. Clearly, the right people are needed to do the training; careful selection of the professional staff is vital. Do not choose individuals who are "all for the cause." Dedication of this sort will be manipulated by the trainee group, who will render these supervisors ineffective. An equally poor course would be the selection of training supervisors who are immature or condescending.

The people to choose, obviously, are those who have the ability to work sympathetically with the trainees, and who are also firm and have the skills and training capability to do the job. They should know something about the problems and background of the trainees. On the other hand, personnel officers who are themselves members of minority groups are often self-conscious about working in programs that involve training the disadvantaged, especially those professionals who are new themselves and are trying to conform to the company's procedures. To assign a person to this specialized position simply because of his race is outrageous. Recently, I talked with a young black accountant who had been taken out of the finance department of a corporation to head a training project for the disadvantaged. It was clear that he had absolutely no interest in or background for the job, nor, for that matter, any choice about the situation. In another instance, a young black woman who had recently completed requirements for her master's degree in counseling and guidance was appointed head of a rather large training program. She had no administrative background to direct an entire program; on the contrary, she was learning from her colleagues.

As a general rule, a firm should not assign the few black professionals on its staff to train the disadvantaged unless they are specially qualified to do so. The use of qualified black personnel can be useful in establishing rapport with the trainees. If the trainer is black as well as "southern gentility" personified, and is only slowly starting to identify with the social changes taking place in the black community, the trainees will know this immediately and will be less receptive to his counsel. Indeed, management should absorb qualified professionals—including those who happen to be minority group members—at all levels.

Approaches in training. Approaches to the trainees must be individualized rather than personalized. This distinction is important, because the trainee is cautious by nature; he hasn't experienced closeness in many areas in his life, and doesn't expect it. On the other hand, most employers believe that a friendly approach is the best way, the way that has worked with employees over the years. The trainers should wait for closeness to occur and let the trainees make the initial moves;

however, note that movement here may not start for months. Address a male trainee by his last name, and a female trainee by "Mrs." or "Miss" followed by the surname. First-name rapports can evolve later. Any woman responsible for children should be addressed as "Mrs." This is not a demand for formality, but it establishes, at least in the beginning, a balanced distance between individuals. Each trainee is an individual, who is aware that he is often regarded by the advantaged person as merely part of a goup. A production line supervisor, talking about the merits of his workers, may use phrases such as "the last bunch you sent me," "take these boys, for example," or "the girls just seem to come and go." These phrases are commonplace and reflect an unconcern for the individual as distinct from equipment, the product, and the schedule.

The tendency to group individuals is a major, and as yet unresolved, problem in special training programs. Present employees must be informed about the program, and the method of imparting this knowledge is important. First of all, sensitivity training sessions should be conducted for department heads, who will be encouraged to see the trainee's point of view, and to question preconceived notions regarding the disadvantaged. It hopefully will contribute to eradicating the stigma that is often attached to programs for the disadvantaged because of the considered "separateness" of the trainees. The department heads then orient the first-line supervisors, who, in turn, have the most difficult task of all: the orientation of the staff employee, who often feels that his job is threatened by the trainees.

The "buddy system." One method of stimulating good morale is the establishment of the "buddy system." In it, an experienced employee—preferably a volunteer—who has had good rapport with his present co-workers is asked to pay particular attention to one trainee, guiding him over the rough spots. The casualness of this relationship is invaluable—the small-talk at lunch, a stroll through other departments, the meeting and greeting of other employees. It may be useful to offer compensation to the veteran employee for this extra effort.

Additional problem situations during the initial program. In addition to the problem situations already mentioned that might be encountered during the initial stages of a training program, some others should be noted. Absenteeism and lack of punctuality frequently characterize undermotivated youth, including school dropouts, as well as those adults who have not developed good attendance and punctuality habits because these disciplines have seldom been demanded of them in the past. Their concept of time is not function- or task-oriented. There will be "no shows" for the initial job interview and "no calls" if absent or late. In these situations, the "buddy" or job coach will discuss the meaning of these requirements and seek out underlying reasons for the lack of response. Even aside from the cost factor, attendance is especially important in a training situation, for one learns on the job by being present, and this daily attendance reinforces other job attainments. In our training experience, it is an ironic fact that those terminated for excessive absenteeism or lateness are invariably persons who can learn the job. Small group sessions attended only by trainees are advisable. Free exchange can take place at these meetings, and the trainees can air their feelings, criticize each other, and reinforce group morale.

Absenteeism is also associated with *active* problems of alcoholism and addiction to hard narcotics (excluding marijuana). Drinking during working hours should not be tolerated. It is a hazard to safe working conditions and often disrupts the efficiency of others. Drug use by an employee involves harsher strictures. A major concern here involves this employee's propensity to steal. Current hourly wage rates alone cannot support the habit of an active hard-drug user. The hiring criteria here should involve the length of time the individual has been drug-free and should also include a review of his efforts to seek employment. Many hard-drug users will be referred by parole or probation officers, whose judgment in such matters is excellent. If the referral is also a released offender, also consider the length of time since release—the longer the better. If the individual qualifies against these guidelines, consider him, not in any lenient fashion, but simply to provide him with a working chance. In any event, if the applicant is a known drug user or has a record, many companies will be unable to offer that chance. Most state laws prohibit banking institutions from hiring anyone with a conviction for theft. Brokerage houses naturally fear the theft of securities (although the degree of fiscal sophistication needed for this would seem to be beyond most disadvantaged persons). In addition, surety firms cannot bond an employee, if it is know that he has a conviction for theft, without a thorough investigation and an eventual rider attached to the blanket liability bond.

After the Training Period

The trainee will develop a sense of pride, like anyone else, after successful completion of the training period. He knows he has achieved; he thereby acquires a sense of success. This is particularly true in the white collar occupations, where trainees tend to place a higher value on status than on take-home pay, because of the earlier pattern of exclusion of minorities from jobs in this field. For example, many young black women refuse to accept high-hourly-rate jobs in the electronics industry as assemblers, but are eager to take significantly lower-paying jobs as clerk-typists. The same pattern exists regarding positions in retail sales. However, there is a growing realization that blue collar jobs are not only better-paying but are also "clean" jobs. Overall, employers of blue collar minority workers must combat a tradition of bitterness toward blue collar and service work, which traditionally has been the only work available to minorities—when work was available; in addition, the minorities have largely been excluded, and often removed, from the higher-paid skilled crafts positions.

For the disadvantaged, the manning chart has been considered a rigid barrier, because graduates of special projects have traditionally been channeled to certain departments only, and avenues of promotion have been limited. However, in expanding job opportunities, do not spotlight the new employee —for instance, through the company newsletter—since it will only bring extra pressures to bear on him.

In closing, I want to note that just as a firm departmentalizes its disadvantaged employees, so I have tried to categorize a variety of characteristics about them. One must ask, however, whether these characteristics automatically presuppose, by definition, a marginal applicant. Even if such a man shapes up with any other average applicant, then merely the unusual care with which he is processed would appear to make him marginal. A case then could be made that white applicants must be hired on a preferential basis, even if "disadvantaged." One overall view appears to be that there is a racially structured suitability factor built into the selection process, and that this is reflected in the placement patterns in most firms. Usually, technical and professional positions for experienced persons are open; but white applicants are favored for administrative, clerical, and production activities. In general, patterns of upgrading after placement in these latter areas generally reflect the present privilege system based on color. Therefore, real change will require your contribution. Assume that no one else will do it, and that the program will have to be continually checked and updated.

One last word. If you really have a go at it, I know how much learning and experience there is to be acquired just for the effort. I only hope your trainees learn one-half what you do.

The Use of Consortiums

Harold W. Phend

Lᴵᴛᴛʟᴇ attention has been given to how medium-size or small firms, able to hire two or five or fifteen hard-core unemployed, can provide for the training of these new employees. Many of these companies cannot afford, even with government assistance, to offer, on their own, programs that must include adult basic education, specialized on-the-job training, and supportive services for a small number of employees. Reluctance to become involved with the government and concern over extra paperwork are cited by businessmen as reasons for their resistance to accepting government aid for training hard-core unemployed. For these firms (as well as for larger companies wishing to hire and train only a small number of employees), consortiums provide an increasingly attractive solution to some of the primary problems.

HAROLD W. PHEND is National Director, Manpower Training Services, Milwaukee, Wisconsin.

The Position of a Consortium

Although accepted by the Department of Labor as legitimate entities for hiring and training the disadvantaged, consortiums have not been widely publicized. Legally, a consortium is a group of individuals or corporations that associate for a specific purpose. In the case of employment programs for the hard-core unemployed, consortiums offer a structure in which many firms can join to negotiate for federal funds while still maintaining their individual identities and arranging their own programs.

To the management of small or medium-size firms, the advantages of grouping together will be obvious. These companies individually have neither the funds nor the facilities for training. In most cases the cost per trainee is too great to train only a few employees, even with government help. Recruiting and paperwork problems can also make a program unrealistic. In a consortium, however, the same firms can work together to receive government funds, pool paperwork and records, and even, if they wish, carry on some aspects of the training together. At the other extreme, companies in a consortium may join together *only* to receive funds, but carry out hiring and training completely separately. The varieties of consortiums are endless, because each partnership can be drawn up to meet the needs of its members, individually and as a unit.

This flexibility is shown in three examples of consortiums operating in the Midwest. One consortium embraces a local department store, a chain of department stores, a tool manufacturer, a firm hiring office personnel, several laundries, an insurance company, and a drugstore chain. These are not all located in the same city. Four of the companies conduct part of their training programs together; the others run separate programs. Another consortium covers 620 jobs in five different cities.

A current Milwaukee consortium involves a partnership of seven companies, with about 85 trainees. Here the Association of Commerce is the consortium sponsor and does the paperwork, but each company has its own program, and each bids for differing amounts of supportive services.

Before detailing how you as an employer can locate or form a consortium and what the federal government will expect to be included in a funded hiring and training program proposal, let us consider a very basic question: Does training the disadvantaged work for *both* the jobless and management? If the answer isn't "Yes," it doesn't matter how amply funded, how progressive, or how well-planned the program is.

In any discussion, then, of financing training programs for the hard-core unemployed, it is relevant to look first at the conclusions of companies that have hired and trained such personnel.

In programs measured by Manpower Training Services, the most successful have had as high as 93 percent retention of employees after a year. In fact, total retention has equaled or is better than that of employees hired through regular personnel department methods. In one case, that of the Wisconsin Telephone Company, of 25 candidates upgraded to meet entry standards in a single program, the company was able to hire 23 deemed unhirable before the special training. This is from a segment of the labor force where normal job retention is two to three months. In an Illinois plant, of 60 employee-trainees unable to pass entry exams and enrolled in special classes at $1.80 an hour, 40 went on to pass and could be placed in jobs earning an average of $3.00 an hour.

The task involves changing an individual with little or no work history, little significant educational achievement, no real understanding of the world he must work and live in, and hostility to much that you try to do for him, into a productive employee. Retention is the critical objective of hard-core unemployed training programs—not just to employ the person, but to give him a place in his community and upward mobility in his job.

For industry much of this program involves tapping new labor markets and developing employees who have been lost to industry because they couldn't be or weren't trained.

It is the experience of firms such as Manpower Training Services, with a good deal of background in the education and training of the disadvantaged, that the company beginning such a program must make a genuine commitment. Hiring and training the hard-core unemployed, with or without government help, is *not* a means of getting cheap labor. It is not enough for the president of a firm to initiate a program because of vague ideas of doing something for the community, and then leave the new employees in dead-end jobs, or worse, help them with education, and then turn them over to supervisors who distrust and dislike them.

Initiating the Program

Once a company has decided to launch a program of hiring and training hard-core unemployed persons, the logical first step is a telephone call or letter to the nearest metropolitan area National Alliance of Businessmen chairman. The NAB has a packet of information for distribution to firms interested in the JOBS (Job Opportunities in the Business Sector) program, and the chairman will be familiar with government financing and what firms and materials are available for a training program.

Where there is proper motivation and understanding on the part of management, and more than 25 employees are involved, a company may want to establish its own hiring and training program, either through its personnel department or through an educational services firm. Employers wanting to hire fewer than 25 workers, and certainly those wanting fewer than 10 people, should discuss consortium possibilities with the NAB metropolitan area chairman. He may refer the employer to the local Chamber of Commerce or contact other community businessmen interested in such a partnership. Because the consortium is a partnership, the lower limit of participating companies is two, but there is no upper limit.

Restrictions on entry. There are some special restrictions on firms entering into consortiums. The firms should all be in the same standard metropolitan statistical area, as defined by the Bureau of the Census. Currently, the Department of Labor is de-emphasizing nationwide consortiums that involve more than one Labor Department region. There must be a relationship between or among companies. Since this is interpreted by the Department of Labor to mean merely participation with an association—even an association formed for that purpose—the government will supply training funds to consortiums formed just for the purpose of negotiating for government funds.

In addition, a firm located near several other companies operating in the same or related fields might prefer to join a consortium with them. Businessmen in a suburb with small but widely divergent industries might join together. The managements of small-town firms might join, possibly using the facilities of a local school for the off-the-job training aspects.

It is possible that a consortium might attract business located in, say, the northwest side of a large city, which would then form the Northwest Association of Manufacturers for the purpose of hiring and training the disadvantaged. A chamber of commerce or trade association might also serve as a sponsor. (Sponsorship will be discussed in the following section.) Frequently, training firms will form consortiums for interested clients, but would prefer not to be the sponsor or prime bidder.

Consortiums are open to all categories of business; however, firms seeking partners will note that the whole hard-core unemployed training and hiring program is inappropriate for companies requiring only highly technical workers and without traditional entry-level jobs.

Naturally, consortiums are faced with many of the same problems that individual firms face when they hold government contracts, but the problems are lessened because they are shared. In fact, there are more restrictions on management's going into a direct contract than there are on consortiums. Credit-rating checks are more detailed, because the government doesn't want to get involved with a firm that may collapse before the contract is fulfilled; a consortium by its nature indicates some stability.

Selection of a sponsor. When two or more interested firms have agreed to enter the field of employing the disadvantaged by contracting for federal funds through a partnership, a sponsor is selected. This sponsor may be one of the companies involved or a trade association. The consortium sponsor holds the prime contract with the government, receives and disburses all moneys to participants and subcontractors, and is responsible for all reporting. All government contracts involve many regulations and no small amount of paperwork (for example, new forms are required for every change in the status of trainees), and because government funds are commonly up to six months late in arriving—during which time training must continue—consortiums frequently prefer to subcontract to a training service. The service then acts as a buffer, making funds available during the delay, receiving and disbursing money, and supplying useful expertise in the reporting.

Proposal to the Department of Labor. After having chosen the sponsor, the consortium, usually guided by the local NAB representative, presents a proposal to the United States Department of Labor. The department then accepts, rejects, or modifies the proposal, which must convince the regional directors that

1. The plan will be well implemented.
2. Participants are sincerely concerned with the program.
3. The plan will help the employee to achieve upward mobility within the company.

The proposal should *not*

1. Merely support an existing program.
2. Train for dead-end jobs.
3. Be a way of getting cheap help.

Consortiums applying for funds must hire within certain standards of eligibility. Those hired as employee-trainees must be poor persons without suitable employment who are—

1. School dropouts.
2. Persons under 22 years of age.
3. Persons 45 years of age or older.
4. Persons who are handicapped with a physical, mental, or emotional condition that could limit work activities.
5. Members of minority groups.
6. Persons subject to special obstacles to employment, such as (a) unskilled workers with two or more periods of unemployment, totaling 15 weeks or more, during the past year; (b) workers whose last jobs were in occupations of significantly lower skill than their previous jobs; (c) workers who have a family history of dependence on welfare; and (d) workers who have been permanently laid off from jobs in industries that are declining in their region.

Terms used in the list of criteria are specifically defined by the government. A person is "poor" if he or she is a member of a family that either receives cash welfare payments or has an annual net income that does not exceed certain amounts in relation to family size and location. For example, the income for a poor family of four living on a farm must not exceed $2,200; but a nonfarm poor family of four must have an income not over $3,200. This income comprises the net cash inflow from all sources by all family members. An income chart for determining eligibility is available through the NAB or the Department of Labor.

Persons without suitable employment include those who are (1) unemployed and available for work, having engaged in a defined variety of job-seeking activities during the preceding four weeks, been waiting to be called back to a job from which they had been laid off, or been waiting to report to a new wage or salary job within the following 30 days (those persons who would technically be classified as "not in the labor force" will be counted as "unemployed" the instant they say they are available for work and are registered as such); (2) underemployed persons, defined as those who are working below their skill capacity, who have received notice that they will be working less than full time in their industries, or who have received notice that they will be unemployed because their skills are becoming obsolete; and (3) those who are not seeking work but should be, including those who would be working or seeking a job if they thought one was available, and those who do not seek work because of motivational problems. Fuller definitions of the eligibility criteria are available through the NAB or the Department of Labor.

The Hiring Program

The program of hiring for on-the-job training and basic education is critical, because management must be reaching out into untapped areas for workers. If the company is not intent on finding jobless men and women and bringing them into the working world to keep them there, then the efforts will be useless.

The unemployed person to be hired and trained by the funds made available to the consortium members may be a functional illiterate but at the same time an exceedingly intelligent adult, able to see through gimmicks—one who knows when he is being "put on." However, he is often so far out of the social mainstream that he doesn't even understand why he should be at work every day. Is he hopeless as an employee? With proper training he can be reached and become a valuable member of the workforce rather than a name on the welfare rolls. When training groups are successfully operated, the turnover rate for the hard-core unemployed is *lower* than the normal job turnover rate.

Hiring standards. Generally the government requires that the consortium or individual firm lower hiring standards.

Therefore, management at hiring locations should keep in mind that the hard-core unemployed often cannot meet the mental aptitude tests or requirements of good work histories without criminal records. There is every indication that properly chosen or trained individuals who failed to meet some of these standards will turn out to be valued employees.

It's especially true that the nonwhite finds job standards a particular frustration. His education may have been totally irrelevant to his needs. Achievement test scores at all grade levels are found to be lower for blacks than for whites, and the gap increases with more years of school. Even high school graduates may find that their education has been inadequate for getting and holding a good job.

A breakdown has been drawn of the hard-core unemployed which, while a generalization, indicates the gulf that can exist between job standards and potentially loyal, efficient employees. This breakdown is as follows: 75 percent male, 25 percent female; 50 percent black, 25 percent Spanish-speaking, and 25 percent white. The median member of the group is married, with three children; lives with 1½ families; eats only two meals per day; averages a sixth-grade education; has no transportation; needs eyeglasses and dental care and has been to a doctor only once in his life; and has been in jail an average of 30 days.

Considering these very real employment barriers, the fact that this is the group from which the consortium companies must be hiring, and the desperate need for employees for entry-level jobs, firms thinking of taking part in a consortium may be interested in the instructions given by one consortium to its hiring staff. The staff was not to let uncommon dress, beards, or "Afro" hairdos reflect unfavorably (unless the characteristic constituted a safety hazard) and was to use common sense in evaluating a candidate's police record. It was suggested that each case be judged on its individual merits.

Costs of the program. Recruiting may be done any way the individual firms in the consortium choose, provided basic requirements are met. But all employee-trainees *must* be certified by either the Concentrated Employment Program (CEP), a federal agency, or the State Employment Service (SES). This leads us into what is one of the biggest problem areas of the JOBS program.

Many people associated with programs for hiring the hard core agree that neither CEP nor SES has contacts or credibility in minority communities. Commonly, teaching services, consortiums, and individual companies have sought out recruits through storefront churches, neighborhood organizations, and so on, and have brought applicants to CEP or SES to be certified. The state or federal agencies then receive credit for finding the trainees. Because of these recruitment difficulties, there is a strong case for the position that consortium sponsors should also be allowed to certify trainees and thus recover some of the cost of recruiting, which is not covered in the government grant.

Costs of a hiring and training program vary, and any estimate is necessarily vague. In general, however, the consortium sponsor may expect that the government will be agreeable within the quite wide limits listed for the various job levels. (Again, the NAB office can supply particulars.) Exclusive of wages, which must meet prescribed levels, the government will pay about 60 percent of the total cost of hiring and training the hard-core unemployed. The remaining 40 percent would be regarded as the normal cost for hiring a new employee and therefore payable by the company or consortium.

In addition, funds are provided for bonding, for some extraneous costs such as production breakage, for minor medical and dental care, for eyeglasses, for some transportation, and possibly for nursery day care for the trainee's preschoolers. How much is covered depends on what is negotiated for.

Despite government help, there are special expenses in hiring totally untrained persons. These costs might be estimated at 10 to 15 percent, maximum, above normal "breaking in" costs. Ordinarily a new file girl needs to be told where the office manual is and where the paper is, and she can begin working. The untrained, perhaps never-before-employed girl needs special attention on the job, which may take more time, temporarily cost more money, and increase some office expenses for a short time.

At this point it is worth repeating that, having accepted a consortium proposal, the government will still take its time about payments. As mentioned earlier, delays of up to six months are common and, as the program goes on, consortium members must be prepared to make funds available themselves, or through their subcontractors, until government money arrives.

Although the consortium sponsor holds the prime contract with the government, the consortium may agree to subcontract some areas of the training, or individual members of the consortium may subcontract portions of their programs. All subcontractors, however, must appear on the original government contracts, or be approved by the Department of Labor.

Consortium proposals for government funds for the hiring and training of the disadvantaged must cover five main areas: counseling, sensitivity training, adult basic education, orientation, and on-the-job training. Currently, consortium members must conduct on-the-job training in the office or plant, although other phases may take place elsewhere.

The Training Program

For either consortiums or individual firms, the basic approaches to job training are to utilize government participation or to proceed on one's own. With either, the firm may select one of three methods: (1) set up the training itself; (2) hire an outside firm; or (3) combine the two.

The drawback in doing it yourself is that most companies do not have the type of talent required for job training for the hard-core unemployed. This is a unique field. It needs new-model experts, willing to innovate and familiar with all that is available. Success or failure is hard to evaluate, and there is a need for people with experience relating to communicating with individuals from the disadvantaged segment of the population.

Programs for JOBS have not all been total successes, although Manpower Training Services is convinced that a properly presented program, either for small companies in a consortium or for the "giants," will bring highly satisfactory results.

In the matter of utilizing government aid, JOBS officials report management concern over the amount of extra paperwork and the fear that government auditors will make frequent visits to their plants to inspect their books.

Although the firm that chooses to conduct the training on its own does have extra paperwork and separate procedures, only the sponsor is responsible for these details in a consortium. Also, some training firms will take on the administrative details, thus completely relieving the consortium of that aspect. Often the amount of government involvement in books is overestimated. Usually only those records directly involved will be checked. Again, if a training firm is involved, its records will be the ones to be checked.

The employer must conduct on-the-job training, because no one knows the particular requirements of a job as well as he; in addition, it is uppermost in the minds of Labor Department officials that a man must be trained for a *specific* job. An important point for consortium members to remember in negotiating for a government contract is that realistic proposals for on-the-job training are expected. To plan for no more training than in normal hiring circumstances is unrealistic. The employer must show that he is aware of difficulties in preparing the disadvantaged for jobs and has specific plans to overcome these difficulties.

Experienced personnel working with training programs recognize that fragmented programs are comparatively ineffective and that stress should be placed on integrated programs wherein counseling, sensitivity training, adult basic education, and orientation are part of a total system. Utilizing plant facilities for all parts of the program is best, for employees can arrive early or stay late on a regular work shift, and they feel more comfortable in familiar surroundings. In addition, the program should be under the complete and full-time direction of one person; the procedure of assigning someone from the personnel department to run the program in addition to his other duties has had poor results.

Sometimes portions of teaching programs can be run from a central "job lab" (such as Manpower's Continuing Education Center in downtown Milwaukee), and if the classes are small enough, with enough individual attention given, and if the atmosphere is relaxed, results can be quite satisfactory. Whether working at an education center or in plants, Manpower Training Services has found a class size of about eight to twelve to be about right for individualized instruction.

Although consortiums may negotiate for and carry out employee education programs themselves, most consortiums prefer to hire subcontractors, or preferably a single subcontractor. Having only one subcontractor to deal with, consortium members see their problems simplified, because the single subcontractor offers the convenience of a central agency. Certainly, hiring a training service firm for any or all members of the consortium has decided advantages. Adult basic education is in its infancy, and the teaching of the disadvantaged is a special discipline, requiring not just the highly educated man or woman, but the person who is "tuned in" to the needs of the disadvantaged, and who has acquired the special skills needed for teaching the disadvantaged. The secret of adult basic education is in the people who do the training more than in their methods, machines, or books. It is in the application of the total system, not in one of its parts.

When consortium members have made plans for on-the-job training and selected (or decided not to select) subcontractors for the other areas, detailed proposals for orientation, adult basic education, counseling, and sensitivity training must be drawn up.

Orientation procedures. Orientation depends on the kind of entry-level jobs being filled, and the key here is *flexibility.* The orientation program must be flexible enough to meet each individual need. It should help to show the new employee the particular job environment and his place in it and seek to help him identify with company interests.

Adult basic education. As mentioned earlier, adult basic education is a specialized field. Currently there are many materials and systems for adult basic education on the market. Many companies, textbook publishers, and training firms supply such things as training materials or even complete training services. In fact, so many firms are "feeling their way" into this field that it is, at best, difficult to understand the merits of what are offered, much less to choose among them. Obviously, they don't all function well. However, whether you are looking for someone to show you the materials with which to conduct your own program, or whether you want to buy an entire package, you as a member of a consortium would do well to remember that adults are not children, and adult education cannot be the same as child education.

Some adults lacking basic reading skills can best be motivated by English taught from modified driver's manuals. This concept isn't as "far out" as it sounds. It brings results. The employee learns basic English and has the pleasure of discovering that he can pass a driver's test!

Is reading and understanding English important? How many accidents in a plant are caused by employees unable to comprehend written safety instructions? The implications of that word "comprehend" are enormous.

Another example of an unusual but practical method is that chosen by a teacher working with Puerto Ricans. Finding they lacked basic English skills and had never experienced a Northern winter, she built their lesson around the items of clothing they would need for the coming frigid weather.

The employee new to the working world often is anxious to quickly make a down payment on a car with his second paycheck. The end result is usually garnishment, or the employee just gets tired of thinking of what he owes and quits. Thus consumer education frequently is part of basic education. The teacher can cover such points as car buying, handling door-to-

86

door salesmen, and watching out for interest rates. While doing this, he can instruct the students in fractions, percentages, and other basic math necessary for particular jobs.

An instructor may find it useful to go over the use of a weekly paycheck with the employee, indicating the various allotments. One teacher who uses this method comments, "At the end, someone will say, 'Where's my couple of bucks for a beer after work?' and we go back to the beginning, and he learns to plan how he can take pocket money out."

Elementary? Certainly, to *you*. But not to a man who's never known a regular income. The goal is that, little by little, he can see himself getting ahead, and can see some point in earning and saving other than to fill immediate needs. For example, his new knowledge of figures may open new doors toward a foreman's job—doors he may not have been able to open before for lack of knowledge; or for the Puerto Rican or Mexican American learning English, the goal might be only to build his self-confidence and to assure him of the company's concern. For disadvantaged people like these, the personal satisfaction of such a simple thing as helping their children with homework is enormous.

Reading comprehension, discussion of civic responsibility, phonics, logic, oral communication—all may be included in a course. Special work in job-related skills is important. Distribution of time and the system of basic education are determined by the nature of the job assigned to the trainee and by his educational needs. Job-related education might be conducted six hours a week or six hours a day. The total system is fully dependent on the employee requirements of each consortium member.

The counseling function. The need for counseling becomes evident when you become aware of the life style of the disadvantaged worker. An employee can be fired for being continually late; a counselor may find that he is late because he doesn't have an alarm clock, or couldn't read the street signs. An employee may suddenly miss many days of work; a counselor may find that he didn't know he needed a heavy winter coat or boots and had no money for them when cold weather arrived. An employee may be performing poorly; a counselor may find that his mind is on the children in his rat-infested home and direct him to an agency to help him find better housing.

The person coming into a firm may have developed in a culture far different from that of his co-workers. This doesn't make him less able, but it may require special methods, as well as patience and understanding. This means counseling for the employee—and human relations training for supervisors and foremen.

Human relations training. Overcoming years of prejudice isn't done in an hour or a week. A beginning is a well-designed course to help the supervisor or foreman understand the mores and culture of the disadvantaged, the problems of minority groups, and the initial limitations of an adult nonworker. It may require time and thought on the part of the foreman to understand that this new worker, if treated with understanding and tact, can become a valuable employee and an asset to the department.

An administrator for Manpower Training Services goes so far as to say that teaching program failures at the firm *usually* come at the supervisory level. He says, "We've put our classroom efforts toward convincing the employee that it is a good company he is working for; then he's turned over to a foreman who shoots it all with one comment: 'I don't want no nigger working on that machine.' "

Maturity of the Program

As employees involved in training programs covered by consortium contracts with the Labor Department change status, the government requires frequent reports. After three to six months a full report must be made covering the whole program, but this is used by the government mainly for research purposes, rather than as a check on the companies. At the end of the term, the sponsor is expected to file a detailed report.

Again, the nearest NAB office can counsel the consortium sponsor on all reporting details.

When the government contract is completed, the consortium is automatically dissolved. Members have had no relation to one another except concerning the specific program; any books and records kept pertain only to the program. There should be no need before, during, or after the life of the consortium for members to have anything to do with the financial affairs of each other's businesses apart from the financial considerations of the consortium.

Firms in a consortium should plan on a partnership of about a year, with most of the education and training figured into the early months. The additional time is necessary for the supportive services, such as counseling, that make the program more effective and offer more permanent results to both the new employees and the companies in the consortium.

Funds for training should continue to be available to private firms in consortiums. The federal government has become dissatisfied with "institutional" training programs, where the unemployed are herded into downtown classrooms and taught to read from "see Dick run" primers or, as in the Concentrated Employment Program, are trained or taught but not necessarily supplied with jobs. It is no secret that in many cases public agencies simply are not solving the problem of the hard-core unemployed. This is not the place to go into the whys of that problem, but they include the forbidding aspect of classrooms for many adults, lack of job-related training, and lack of understanding of the varieties of adult motivations.

As a result, more money is being made available to employers who promise both the job and the training. Under the Nixon administration, indications are that the Department of Labor will continue to award funds under the amended Manpower Development and Training Act of 1962 and the Economic Opportunity Act of 1964 and that more funds will be available as institutional programs are further de-emphasized.

The current Labor Department program, MA-5, is the most flexible design yet, with greatly expanded options. Option A (pertaining to training for the new employees) remains largely the same as in previous programs. However, Option B allows for upgrading of present employees in order to release entry-level jobs for the disadvantaged.

Why get involved in hiring the hard-core unemployed at all when you need only a few men? If you've got recruiting problems and if the available workforce can't meet your entry standards, you're in trouble whether you need 5 men or 50. Traditional recruiting methods are aimed at people who, in today's labor market, already have rewarding jobs and see little need to change. A solid hiring-training program for the unemployed, especially in a consortium situation, may be more efficient in terms of both time and money.

The MA-5 program has opened the field of upgrading current employees to consortiums, and it is interesting to consider some figures in this area. One way to make use of potentially efficient workers now being completely lost to industry is to make entry-level jobs available for the currently unemployed by upgrading employees now locked into those jobs. Some benefits of upgrading the employees you already have are immediately apparent. But its effects on productivity are not well known. Employees in a medium-size plant were noted to be working at 70 percent efficiency before an upgrading program went into effect. Following training, their rates were charted at 138 to 140 percent!

In closing, it should be noted that the social motive behind any firm's entering into a consortium concerned with the hard-core unemployed simply can't be discounted. It's vital. As you think in terms of solving your employee problems, you may also wish to take a hard look at your business neighborhood, at the kind of facilities your employees live with, at the contribution you and your firm could make. The interest and involvement of the employer can be instrumental in the success of employees finding their way in today's world.

A Municipal-Industrial Venture: The Woodland Job Center

Albert D. Cunningham, Jr.

Cleveland is a city in which East and West are divided both physically and psychologically by the Cuyahoga River. In spite of many bridges, the two sides are worlds apart. The East Side is essentially black, and with the exception of a branch of the Community College, embodies most of the universities and traditional cultural centers. The West Side is primarily composed of bedroom communities, ethnically organized. On the West Side there is a multiplicity of single-family dwellings and relatively few apartment buildings; the East Side, on the other

ALBERT D. CUNNINGHAM, JR. is General Manager, Woodland Job Center, Cleveland, Ohio.

hand, has many multiple dwellings and is commonly considered to contain the inner core or ghetto areas, the most notorious of which is Hough.

The Cuyahoga River presents more than a physical barrier. It also represents a contrast in life styles and ideologies. Neither side tends to be too familiar with the terrain of the other side. West Siders who wander past the downtown Public Square tend to be completely lost on the East Side. East Siders are completely disoriented on the West Side. A spirit of apprehension tends to prevail on each side toward the other. That most of these fears are groundless is not really relevant, since reality is in the mind of the beholder. This "distance" between the two sides could pose some fairly interesting problems for the Woodland Job Center, which is located on the East Side, but is intended to serve the Cleveland metropolitan area.

Dr. Paul W. Briggs, Superintendent of the Cleveland Public Schools, described Cleveland as:

> . . . a city where the extremes of affluence and poverty are found but where poverty is spreading at an alarming rate. It is a city characterized by too much isolation—racial, ethnic, religious, social, and economic. It is a city whose daily newspapers list column after column of good jobs waiting to be filled, while unemployment in the inner city is among the nation's highest. It is a city where we annually lose 4,000 young people as school dropouts—unprepared for any productive role in the economy. It is a city where $50 million is spent on relief in one year, a city where one out of four families lives in a rat-infested dwelling, a city with 50,000 adult functional illiterates and where 45 percent of the population over 21 has not gone beyond the eighth grade.[*]

[*] Remarks by Paul W. Briggs, Superintendent, Cleveland Public Schools, at meeting of National Industrial Conference Board, January 10, 1968.

Development of the Program

The concerns mentioned by Dr. Briggs were shared by the industrial leaders of Cleveland. Mr. Ralph Besse, board chairman of Cleveland Electric Illuminating Company and the Cleveland Inner City Action Committee, was approached by Mr. Robert V. Corning, general manager of General Electric's Lamp Division, to discuss the dilemma. Out of these discussions came the decision to involve school officials in an effort to unite the competences and resources of education and industry in breaking the poverty-welfare cycle in the inner city. General Electric owned a 4½-acre, three-story warehouse on Cleveland's predominantly black East Side. The warehouse, estimated to cost $5 million to duplicate, was donated to the school system.

Dr. Briggs' endorsement of the concept of a cooperative venture sponsored jointly by education and industry received enthusiastic support from the business community leaders. He received some initial funding for planning and staffing from local and national foundations, including Educational Facilities Laboratories of New York, The Codrington Foundation, and the Martha Holden Jennings Foundation.

The Greater Cleveland Growth Association (GCGA) in cooperation with the National Alliance of Businessmen (NAB) and the Cleveland Public School System joined in the development of a plan to attack the interrelated problems of school dropouts, unemployment, poverty, and manpower shortages. The basic purpose of the plan was to provide unemployed inner-city residents with vocational and on-the-job training that would enable them to function successfully as regular employees of industry and business.

The U.S. Department of Labor encouraged business and industry to submit proposals for funding of training contracts. These could be individual, consortium, or national contracts. In a series of meetings among the Cleveland Public Schools GCGA, and representatives from the private sector, it became clear that the formation of a consortium was in the offing. It was decided to shoot for an MA-3 contract with the U.S. Department of Labor under the consortium format. This decision required finding solutions to several problems: job development, recruitment procedures, training and supportive services, placement—on-the-job training, and maintenance and follow-up.

Job development. The job development was accomplished by the NAB. By canvassing their colleagues and associates they secured 1,050 job commitments from 77 companies. To qualify for the MA-3 contract the commitments needed only to be translated into specific job titles and descriptions. This required that employers be as definitive as possible in their descriptions and that the proposal writers be relentless in their use of the Dictionary of Occupational Titles.

Employee-trainees were to be hired by industrial and business firms that had made commitments to the Growth Association through the NAB. These job slots went into the GCGA's proposal to the U.S. Department of Labor.

Recruitment procedures. Employee-trainees were to be recruited from among residents who were members of minority groups, were unemployed or underemployed, were poor, and lived in Cleveland's inner city.

Trainees were to be recruited directly and by Cleveland's Concentrated Employment Program (CEP) AIM-Jobs, supplemented by the Ohio Bureau of Employment Services, CEP Neighborhood Centers, county welfare agencies, and private agencies. Recruiting, coaching, counseling, and follow-up procedures were geared to make the greatest possible use of subprofessionals recruited from the same areas of the inner city. This was in the cooperative spirit of the overall venture.

An important feature of the program was that each employee-trainee would be on the payroll of a business or industry as soon as he or she entered the Woodland Job Center.

An orientation program at AIM-Jobs familiarized employee-trainees with the total program and its relevance as a means by which they could gain worthwhile and profitable employment. This phase at AIM-Jobs helped determine work readiness, advised the employee-trainee of his role in job success, and prepared him for his entry into the Center on an employer's payroll.

During the AIM-Jobs orientation period, an assessment was made of each employee-trainee's current needs in terms of educational, health, and social skill characteristics. Aptitude, interest, and personality assessments were made by the counseling staff as a basis for hand-tailoring an individualized remediation and developmental program for each employee-trainee. The orientation that began at AIM-Jobs was continued throughout the program under the direction of the Center's advisers. There was also a free exchange of information.

Training and supportive services. Each employee-trainee was scheduled into basic and/or remedial education classes, job experiences, and supportive services on the basis of individual needs, skills, aptitudes, and background. Each progressed through the program at the Center at his own rate of speed.

The success of the program, in terms of developing employable individuals who can hold onto a job successfully, is closely related to the effectiveness with which the attitudes and self-images of individuals can be changed. Consequently, a combination of financial incentives, relevant training experiences, and supportive conditions formed the program's strategy for change. The orientation, vocational, and on-the-job training experiences were designed to convey to the employee-trainee a feeling of personal accomplishment.

The philosophical orientation of the program stemmed from the belief that the employee-trainees possess considerable amounts of undeveloped potential. If appropriate training and supportive experiences could be organized, positive changes in attitudes, achievement, and motivation could result. Since the process of changing human behavior is not a conveniently packaged product, the program was designed to maximize flexibility in terms of organization and presentation of training experiences. Every effort was made to organize training and supportive resources to make it possible for participants to taste success through unmistakable personal accomplishment.

In order to insure that staff personnel at the training center and at business and industrial sites were prepared to work with the employee-trainees, provisions were made to increase both awareness and competence of the staff personnel to work with hard-core unemployed, disadvantaged residents of the city. The staff visited work sites and planned programs with employer representatives.

After diagnosis of the needs of each employee-trainee, an individual course of action was planned by Center staff. It was anticipated that communication skills, arithmetic, and social skills required on the job should receive emphasis. This emphasis in all training phases was placed on practical applications. Remedial reading and arithmetic were related to prevocational and social skill training. Instructional groups were organized in units of approximately ten employee-trainees per instructor. Tutoring and individualized instruction were provided where small-group instruction was not effective.

Each employee-trainee was taken progressively from the level of readiness and academic know-how that he had brought to the Center to one that would enable him to function effectively as a regular employee.

Since hard-core unemployed have experienced frequent failure in relation to job requirements, supportive services in terms of counselors and specialized staff were available to redirect potential failure experiences into success situations.

In most instances, the participants did not have successful work histories; consequently, typical instructional strategies would not bring about the behavioral changes needed for sustaining employment.

Critical to the selection of instructional methods was the realization that most dropouts and hard-core unemployed do not view themselves as being able to achieve. Evidence indicates that nonachieving individuals tend to see their lives as being controlled by external events and forces. Acceptance of this philosophy tends to create a negative self-image that stands as an obstacle to acquiring basic skills and becoming a self-generating person. In light of this realization, instructional methods

96

were selected and organized to develop attitudes leading to self-success and intrinsic motivation.

The instructional design finally decided upon can be stated as follows:

1. A diagnostic assessment of personal, vocational, and educational needs will be made for each individual. Testing occurs only after the trainee is hired. This helps dispel the trainee's fear of being tested for exclusion.
2. This diagnosis will serve as a basis for the development of an individually prescribed employment and training plan or experience.
3. Instruction will be organized in small groups of not more than ten and conceivably less than five individuals who display similar learning dysfunctions.
4. Time and space factors will be guided by the specifically diagnosed needs of individuals without regard to traditional class schedules.
5. Instructional facilities will include a full complement of projectors, Learning Masters, Tachistoscopes, and appropriate mechanical aids to maximize motivation and reinforce learning experiences.
6. Individualized instruction will be made possible through use of tutorial procedures to reinforce and support where needed.
7. Instructional materials will be selected and developed to insure adequate levels of difficulty, high interest, and relevance of content and appearance.
8. It will be the responsibility of advisers to evaluate progress each week for each trainee so that appropriate alterations and additions can be made to the individualized training program.
9. A learning specialist will be available to the staff and curriculum development groups to insure that both human development and learning theory are utilized in the formulation of instructional methods.

Course content was organized around behavioral objectives in which traditional tasks were taught in a more relevant context. For example:

> Given an hourly rate, the trainee can compute the net earnings for his set of circumstances.

This objective has many facets, each of which might be a lesson. The computation skills required constitute an excellent review of addition, subtraction, multiplication, and division as the basis for remedial work.

> The trainee chooses a mode of verbal communication appropriate to the situation in which he finds himself.

It seems fairly apparent that many language levels are present in our society. It was also interesting that the trainees, themselves, possessed and used several. This approach permitted and encouraged trainees to use their verbal skills. It also oriented them to expectations of employers.

> The trainee can define the parameters of his role as an employee.

A working knowledge of his job description enables the employee-trainee to avoid misunderstandings. It also forces employers to be more definitive in describing jobs. The point at which both employee and employer are looking at the same reality is the beginning of a meaningful relationship.

Placement—on-the-job training. Since the trainees would be the hired employees of a company, the placement phase was already accomplished. However, many problems arose that had not been anticipated. Some companies were located in remote places. Even if the trainee could get to work, getting home by public transportation was impossible unless he drove. Very few trainees had access to cars. One instructor left the Center at 2:00 P.M. His assignment was to get to the plant in time for the

4:00 P.M. shift using public transportation. It took him 2½ hours, and the last leg was a 17-block walk. Program design required a car pool "buddy" system for that company. In other instances shift changes were necessary so that public transportation would be available.

Placement also included, or required, on-the-job training for some companies. Small companies or concerns with only a few trainees were hard-pressed to duplicate work experience at the Woodland Job Center. Employee-trainees had to receive an average of eight weeks of on-the-job training after completion of Center orientation at the work site. The on-the-job training could be at the employer's location or at the Woodland Job Center, where certain employers could organize and maintain a miniproduction facility. The development of Center work sites met with reluctance from employers. The capital outlay for personnel, equipment, and the logistics of moving material could not be taken lightly. To date, only five companies have chosen this route, and only General Electric has maintained a continuous operation. The others sponsored one or two groups and are now evaluating the results.

On-the-job training was conducted at various sites throughout Cleveland. Generally, employee-trainees spent eight weeks in vocationally related training at the Woodland Job Center and eight weeks in on-the-job training activities in an employer's plant or business or at the Center. In those instances in which an employee-trainee reached a level of readiness that enabled him to function effectively in an on-the-job training situation, he entered the on-the-job training before the expiration of the eight weeks. Therefore, the amount of time spent at the Center in vocationally related training was decreased, thus expanding the on-the-job training.

During the on-the-job training period, the Center was responsible for the supportive services for each employee-trainee. Observations and conferences were held at least once a week. The conferences were held separately between or among counselors, employee-trainees, and appropriate employees of the companies who were providing the on-the-job training.

Of the 1,050 job commitments secured by GCGA through NAB from 77 companies, approximately 400 firm job slots with 37 companies materialized for Center training. Some commitments were filled directly by companies, the CEP, and other agencies. A few failed to materialize because of skepticism, and others were withdrawn because of changes in the company's outlook. In only one instance were trainees laid off (the loss of a major contract precipitated this action). The trainees, although disappointed, went to work for other companies.

Maintenance and follow-up. The CEP was designed so that after two weeks of orientation, job coaches would follow their trainees to the work sites. Since the CEP had been in operation for about two years before the Woodland Job Center came into existence, many companies were already dealing with the coaches and referring problems to them. In the initial planning it was agreed that when a coach was assigned to a company, the Center would not duplicate this personnel.

It soon developed that the eight-week stay at the Center had a more profound counseling effect on the trainees than the two-week orientation at the CEP. Seemingly, the Center advisers had established rapport with our clients. Also, all the people coming into the Center did not come through the CEP. This meant that the Center advisers had to follow up on the progress of some of the trainees in spite of the prior presence of a CEP coach.

It took the Center advisers weeks of trial and error to establish the problem referral system. In the beginning some trainees lost their jobs because of absence, tardiness, or other reasons, before the Center knew they were having difficulty. However, as the Center developed contacts within companies, its track record for trainee job maintenance improved considerably. A follow-up questionnaire was mailed in June 1969 to the first 307 trainees who had come through the Center.

Over the next 2½ months we recovered 301 questionnaires, from 232 men and 69 women. Most of the questionnaires were returned by mail; Center advisers traced the balance by phone and by personal visits. The most significant information gleaned from this effort was as follows:

- A total of 40 percent of the new employees still had their original jobs.
- In spite of approximately 30 percent quitting and 20 percent being fired, 70 percent of all trainees remained in the workforce.
- A total of 50 percent of the men and over 60 percent of the women had received one or more raises.

In this regard it should be noted that the average starting wage was $2.10 for men and $1.65 for women. More women received raises than did men.

The feedback from our trainees tends to indicate that the contacts the new worker makes in the workaday world are supportive; they help guide him into better positions.

As of October 1969, the Center's overall record included

Enrollment to date	435
Separations because of poor performance	42
Separations because of illness, moving, incarceration	22
Placements in jobs	335
Current enrollment	36

Training Options

With a consortium of diverse employers, no single training format was possible. Planning meetings between the employers and the Center staff helped to overcome some of the misgivings concerning the hard core and lessened some of the employers' apprehensions about working with school people. Probably our most saving grace was that we didn't pretend to know everything, and we were eager to learn about businesses.

The first decision to be worked out was a distribution of the trainee time while at the Center. Frequently, the employer "wanted 'em softened up" before he became involved. Usually we were able to work out a more equitable arrangement, with the trainee spending increasingly more time with the employer. Some trainees were expected to go to work immediately! Since the Center's efforts were to be supportive of the employer's job, the trainee needed to perform real work as soon as possible. It was the feeling of the Center's staff that the trainee should not become overly adjusted to "Center life" and then be confronted by the new situation. The number of trainees an employer had had no bearing on the time distribution selected. As a result of dealing with nearly 40 employers and approximately 400 trainees, the Center worked with the following variety of schedules:

TRAINEE TIME DISTRIBUTION OPTIONS

Option	Center Staff	Employer Personnel
A	½ day mornings	½ day afternoons
B	½ day afternoons	½ day mornings
C	½ day M; T; ½ W; Th	½ day M; ½ W; F
D	½ day M; T; ½ W; Th; ½ F	½ day M; ½ W; ½ F
E	M; W; F	T; Th
F	T; Th	M; W; F
G	Even weeks	Odd weeks
H	Odd weeks	Even weeks

Fortunately, there were rarely more than five to seven groups involved at any given time. After the employer's personnel became familiar with the members of his group, he would frequently elect to work with the trainees at the Center instead of having them come to him. This, of course, involved changes in the time distribution formats.

Finding a Consortium

One of the characteristics of our business-industrial system is that we organize and reorganize, group and regroup, define and redefine phenomena. Not infrequently the new group is comprised of all the old members; the new organization is practically identical to its predecessor; and the problem is age-old. Unemployment, welfare, housing, education, medical care, crime, and a host of other urban social concerns have been dealt with under various names, auspices, and philosophical persuasions. A novel feature of this war on unemployment is that its eradication is being tackled by both the public and the private sectors. Indeed, the Chamber of Commerce, National Alliance of Businessmen, Job Opportunities in the Business Sector, Economic Opportunity Agency, Concentrated Employment Program, and Cooperative Area Manpower Planning System in most cities are, in reality, different names for the same sector.

The Cleveland consortium was drawn essentially from the same group, the big difference being that participation was encouraged by peers as opposed to its being a response to pressure from some civic-minded group or groups. It would appear that such cooperative support is the better method of recruiting participating employers. One would conclude that an employer can seek assistance from a rather sizable continuum—from the Chamber of Commerce to a craft guild. A note of caution must be interjected at this point. Because of the difficulty involved in recruiting people, advantaged or disadvantaged, who possess the mental and/or physical dexterity to succeed in a specific industry, and because of the difficulty in training people who have had no previous exposure to an employer's area, it appears somewhat temeritous to attempt training in a consortium ranging from acetylene welding to zipper repair.

It seems as though the most efficient groupings cluster about business-industrial organizations: associations, guilds, societies, and so forth. This is especially true of the small-shop employer. In concert with similar enterprises, a shop with limited facilities and resources can contribute and benefit without shouldering the entire burden. It is somewhat axiomatic that the greatest deterrent is internal squabbling over the fruits of the combined effort. Assessing input—that is, equipment, material, and personnel—in order to assign benefit priorities tends to be the greatest hangup. However, it is not unmanageable.

Another approach is for large concerns to assume a somewhat benevolent role, whereby the fruits of their efforts are shared with the smaller concerns. This is somewhat idealistic and is not likely to occur in the foreseeable future.

Financing the Program

Under the MA-3 format, participating companies and agencies can be reimbursed under the fixed unit cost provision of the contract. This reimbursement is for extraordinary cost and is described as follows by the Department of Labor:

> The fixed unit cost assistance request you submit for each job title should reflect only a portion of the *extraordinary costs,* that is, only the costs over and above those customarily incurred by an employer in hiring and training a new employee. For example, costs considered for submission might include a portion of the difference of the cost of orienting and counseling an ordinary trainee and orienting and training a hard-core disadvantaged trainee.†

> Contracts can be up to 24 months. There is no minimum. However, it is important to remember that reimbursement of the fixed cost will be made on a minimum 12-months basis. For example, the fixed unit cost is determined by dividing the total cost of training by 260 (260 is the number of working days in a year based on a five-day week.) Thus all repayment cycles are based on a 12-month cycle.‡

> Any extraordinary training and/or rehabilitation costs needed to train the hard-core worker to be fully productive may be borne by the government. This includes, but is not limited to, educational training services, medical and dental

† U.S. Department of Labor, Manpower Administration, *Supplemental Information for the Preparation of JOBS/MA-3 Proposals* (April 1968), p. 10.
‡ Ibid., p. 17.

exams, transportation, counseling, productivity differentials, and certain other additional costs such as administrative expenses, sensitivity training for supervisors, et cetera, [which] are allowable.§

An illustration of typical program services and components:
A. Orientation
   1. Medical and dental examination and services
   2. Initial testing and counseling
   3. Basic job-related orientation
B. Job-Related Basic Education
   1. Special counseling and testing
   2. Prevocational education
   3. Basic skill preparation
C. On-the-Job Training
   1. Skill training
   2. Special counseling
   3. Wastage, equipment breakage
   4. Productivity differential
D. Administrative Cost and Overhead
   1. Transportation
   2. Supervisory and co-worker orientation
   3. General administration and overhead¶

One of the hazards for employers and the participating agencies was that each employee-trainee was considered a funded line. A dropout could be replaced, but only the *unused* portion of the fixed unit cost was available for reimbursement for the "new" trainee. Since the initial cost to the employer was the most expensive period of his participation, a "lost" employee-trainee was also a financial loss. If the employer elected *not* to replace the trainee, the employer, along with the participating agencies, received only that portion of the fixed unit cost that covered the period of the trainee's employment. All employers would prefer a cost-plus arrangement.

§ Ibid.
¶ Ibid., p. 11.

Sensitivity Training

The basic approach to sensitivity training has its emphasis on improving the awareness of supervisors. The Center's experience indicates that trainees hold tenaciously to a number of half-truths and preconceived ideas. Because of the Center's commitment to a cooperative program with business, the employer's personnel are never abandoned by the Center's staff to shift for themselves among the trainees until after we have planned and executed several joint activities. This requires observing trainees together in both shops and classes, and fosters better communication among trainees, foremen, instructors, and advisers. In some instances this is the first interaction some participants have had with other ethnic groups.

The indications are that a *task*-oriented exercise does more to overcome cultural and communication barriers than any amount of round-table discussions. In most discussion situations between trainees and supervisory people, the situation seems to do more to reinforce old feelings than to provide a new base for possible cooperation.

One of the first companies to install a workshop at the Center assigned a very knowledgeable man as foreman. After several planning meetings some of his fears began to subside until he interviewed his potential trainees. He then found that our mutual planning of shop and class activities was useful to him. He accepted the suggestion not to post a list of rules but to let the group of trainees help in their formulation and adoption. Immediately upon entering the shop, the trainees were instructed in a total of three jobs and assigned to work stations. The jobs involved the disassembling and reassembling of a rather delicate piece of electrical equipment. Inputs from the foreman's plant colleagues led him to order what he thought were sufficient materials for six of the trainees to work on for five weeks. To his amazement, they completed the work, with exceptional quality, in less than two weeks. In the process the workers and the foreman learned to accept and to respect each other.

The NAB has sponsored a series of one-day sensitivity-orientation workshops at the Woodland Job Center. The workshops' materials and activities were developed by the Human Development Institute, a division of Bell & Howell. Employers are encouraged by the NAB metro chairman to send the first-line supervisors who will be working directly with the disadvantaged. To date, at least a dozen workshops have been held. The participants all seem to appreciate the help. Those supervisors who have been through the workshop, and have come to the Center planning meeting, are considerably better informed and much easier to work with. It also appears that they are more easily acclimated to working with the target population.

Woodland Enterprises and the Shop Program

The original cooperative concept at Woodland included provisions for companies to establish production shops at the Center. The cost of installing a company's facility was to be jointly shared by the Cleveland Board of Education and the company, with the equipment and materials remaining the property of the company. What was needed was a mechanism that would legally permit this relationship. Dr. Briggs, Superintendent of Schools, solicited the counsel of a prominent Cleveland law firm. Concurrently, the Center administration was meeting with representatives of companies interested in participation. The original intent to work together was broadened and refined to include the nuts and bolts of a real business operation.

A major concern of companies was to avoid violation of their union agreements. Anyone they hired would be under these agreements, and it was felt that there were too many unknowns for this kind of involvement. Another problem was the shop-class time distribution. On the basis of our experience with trainees in the consortium, we learned that the emphasis should be placed squarely on the work aspect of the program. The tendency of some employers was to opt for a split day:

half shop, half classes. Legally, the school system could not pay students (trainees). Yet the trainee-employees had to be paid if we were going to attract workers.

In January 1969, the Articles of Incorporation were filed with the Secretary of State at Columbus, Ohio. In February, the Board of Education of the Cleveland City School District passed a resolution authorizing the superintendent to enter into an agreement with Woodland Enterprises. Woodland Enterprises was authorized by this agreement to

- Provide special instruction urgently needed in the school district.
- Use appropriate portions of the building and grounds at 4966 Woodland Avenue.
- Maintain premises and any equipment in good condition and repair.
- Bear all cost in connection with space occupied.
- Remodel with the consent of the authorized district representative.
- Vacate the premises at the option of the district.
- Save the district from all damages that might occur, whether to a person or persons on the premises occupied or used by Woodland Enterprises.
- Comply with all federal, state, and local laws, ordinances, rules, and regulations that from time to time might be applicable to Woodland's use and occupancy.**

In March, the trustees of Woodland Enterprises elected a president, secretary-treasurer, and assistant secretary-treasurer.

A new kind of organization emerged that could assume responsibility for nearly all the functions heretofore performed by several dispersed agencies. Woodland Enterprises, by having its operational base at the Woodland Job Center, can now

** Official Proceedings of the Board of Education of the City of Cleveland School District, Cuyahoga County, Ohio, February 25, 1969, p. 63.

108

provide one-stop service to clients. It also has access to the resources of both the Cleveland school system and the business-industrial community. The Ohio Bureau of Employment Services (OBES) has office space and does the recruiting. Pre-employment physicals are administered by the school's health service. Woodland Enterprises hires the trainees; assigns them to shops (three shops are operating at this writing); administers the hourly wage program; schedules academic classes; counsels; and participates in the periodic performance reviews that lead to job placement with the company that has the training shop.

The basic program is eight hours a day, five days a week, for eight weeks. During the first four weeks, employee-trainees attend classes eight hours a week: two hours a day for four days. In the fifth and sixth weeks they are in classes two hours a day, three days a week. During the last two weeks, the employees work full time.

The Woodland Enterprises employees are paid on the basis of 40 hours per week—less, of course, any time lost because of absence or tardiness. From the first day, they can earn a $0.10 per hour bonus by coming every day, on time. Since the minimum wage is $1.60 per hour, this means that they can earn $1.70 through their own effort from the beginning. If an employee loses his bonus by being absent or late during the week, he is again eligible for the bonus the following week. Students are counseled as need arises. Most adviser-employee conferences center around tardiness, absence, domestic problems, health, and legal entanglements. Advisers are not limited to working at the Center, and they frequently go to the trouble site, whether it is class, shop, home, job, or jail. All employees are reviewed every two weeks with the shop foremen, instructors, advisers, and the Woodland Enterprises administration. At each employee's second review, some projection is made in terms of job readiness.

Since the shop experience exposes the Woodland Enterprises employees to a variety of the company's operations, the company increases its latitude in placement. When the Woodland Enterprises employee is evaluated as job-ready, he is channeled into the company's employment procedure. Usually this consists of an interview at the Center with the Company's employment personnel, who make the job offer. The interviewer has access to the potential employee's work record at Woodland Enterprises. In many instances, this may be not only the longest work record the applicant has but his only work record.

General Electric's Cleveland Lamp Division has operated such a shop at the Center since March 1969. The foreman and the mechanic are General Electric personnel. The equipment and materials also belong to the company.

Companies stipulated that the facility should include such services as utilities, janitorial service, and guard duty. They were willing to pay reasonable rates for these services. They also indicated that they would be more comfortable with control of the trainee input and output of their shops. This was reasonable, since their need for new employees would vary according to fluctuations in the marketplace.

A pitfall to be avoided was providing trainees with an industrial experience in the hope of placing them with nonparticipating companies. Conceivably, we may work up to that, but it appeared prudent not to rely on such providence at the outset.

The wage range scale discussions indicated that unless the trainee could start at or above the minimum wage, the program would immediately lose some of its attractiveness. A minimum wage for beginning trainees as well as increments to reward improving performance heightened the anticipation of success for all concerned. It was also suggested that all participating companies agree to use the prescribed pay scale.

There was total agreement that the shops should be staffed and operated by company personnel and that the instructors and advisers should have in-service training in the shops.

What evolved was the need for a third-party, nonprofit corporation. Six community leaders from business, industry, foundations, unions, and the press were contacted by Dr. Briggs to become the trustees; all accepted. Conceptually, Woodland Enterprises was born.

There are nine production operations conducted in the shop in addition to logistical functions. Trainees rotate through job stations and perform all tasks necessary to the shops' operation. The results, thus far, look promising and encouraging:

	Men	Women	Total
Enrollment to date	26	28	54
Voluntary terminations	6	2	8
Involuntary terminations	6	0	6
Placements	9	18	27
Discharges after placement	3	2	5
Current enrollment	6	7	13

Seven of the male losses, because of involuntary terminations and discharges after placement, occurred early in the program. Since then our holding power has improved considerably. Most of this improvement is attributed to the inclusion of more tasks that the male workers consider masculine. Also, the women seem more amenable to handling small production items.

A Language Training
Program: Tenneco Chemicals

Stephen G. Harrison

The kaine that I do is machine operator. Every day I came
to work at seven o'cloch in the mounig. I start to work raigh
whan I pank out de cart. At nine o'cloch take the brike
and then I com to the school. At 12 achark in the moaning
I have lonch. What am do in home—am go home from the
work and I take a bath and then . . . .

LUIS did not finish, or could not finish, or would not
finish. It was the same way on the factory floor—not necessarily
with Luis, but with enough Spanish-speaking employees that
General Foam Division of Tenneco Chemicals, Inc. was having all it could do to obtain a week's production, accurately

STEPHEN G. HARRISON is Manager, Industrial Relations, General
Foam Division, Tenneco Chemicals, Inc., New York.

processed and accurately shipped. It was not because Luis and most of his fellow employees were poor workers or lacked motivation; it was because they somehow simply did not, or could not, or would not understand. And sometimes when they did not understand they were afraid to *say* that they did not understand. This made the problem almost impossible.

The strained attempt by Luis to write a composition about his typical work day took place in an English class—not given at school, but right in his own factory, by a multilingual language instructor, employed by Luis's company for just that purpose. It was Luis's first class, and even though the teacher wrote,

> . . . you are doing very well, Luis. Try to concentrate on improving spelling. . . .

Luis knew that he had a long way to go. But Luis, like almost all Latins, was a proud person. To work in an American factory where the pace was fast and the margin for error was slight was enough of an exercise in self-control for any new employee. Compound the problem with an employee born and bred in a Latin culture, under a markedly different socioeconomic environment, speaking a foreign language and having resided with his family in the vibrant northeastern United States for just a short time, and the problem of molding a well-coordinated workforce becomes an imposing one indeed.

The Role of Tenneco's General Foam Division

General Foam, aside from being the largest division of Tenneco Chemicals, Inc., is a supplier of polyether urethane foams for the furniture and bedding industries, polyester foams for textile uses, and a variety of related products for industrial and consumer applications. Its expansion in New Jersey has taken place almost entirely since 1966, until there now are four manufacturing sites (Carlstadt, East Rutherford, Moonachie, and

Rockaway). The company's other domestic locations are in Hazelton, Pennsylvania—a facility employing seven hundred persons—and New York City, its divisional headquarters. The expansion in New Jersey has taken place with a workforce composed predominantly (as high as 80 percent) of Spanish-speaking hourly workers. These are mainly Cuban and Puerto Rican.

The tales of woe being told by most established New Jersey employers who desperately seek hourly workers are echoed in almost every industrial county and industrial park in the northern part of the state. Usually the market is very tight, and even when an employer is fortunate enough to have a full complement of employees so that he may realistically produce at his plant's capacity, he finds his turnover and absenteeism problem to be nearly the last straw. The never-ending one-up-manship commonly manifested by employers in an effort to carve out their employee requirements from personnel of other companies could stimulate the imagination of any student of personnel practices. General Foam has found itself in the thick of this.

Although time spent going through the strenuous employment exercises is bound to bear some fruit if the personnel departments work long enough and hard enough, it seemed to J. P. Lamb, director of personnel and industrial relations at Tenneco Chemicals, and to the divisional management at General Foam, that such an effort is not permanently constructive. For all the contortions gone through to hire a handful of workers, there was too much time involved to permit attention to be given to an equally important problem: What can be done to be sure that most of the employees obtained from the employment market will remain with the company, and will prefer this company over others with similar benefits? Would it not be a more prudent investment in time and money to create a condition at the workplace wherein the difficult recruitment of employees with sound language skills was no longer necessary? Indeed, would it not be an attractive goal for General Foam, which has an equal opportunity program for both labor and

114

management personnel, to augment this by welcoming the employment of all disadvantaged groups, including newly arrived Latins with virtually *no* language skills?

Background of the program. Such notions remained dormant until the spring of 1969, when a combination of events led to the decision to hire a full-time language instructor.

First, a representative of the National Alliance of Businessmen's JOBS program visited General Foam's New York facility to evaluate the successes and failures of the company's experiment in this area. He encouraged new ideas to expand the employment potential of the disadvantaged. Second, the training that had to be done during that year to facilitate the scale-up of the Moonachie and Rockaway plants was being frustrated by the language barrier. Third, and most important, the company's human relations conferences—bimonthly labor-management meetings attended by representatives at all levels on both sides—provided the proper forums. It was here that *any* subject was acceptable for discussion except one involving interpretation of the language of the labor contract (subjects of this nature were reserved for the grievance machinery). Roy Soden, executive board member and director of Region No. 8, International Union of District 50, UMWA, had the union represented by field representative Manuel Mirailh—himself originally from Puerto Rico.

The decision for language training. At the outset of a human relations conference in April 1969, it became clear that not even the beautiful luncheon that preceded the meeting was enough to break the tension that permeated the room. The Spanish-speaking representatives, through Mr. Mirailh, made it clear that they were frustrated with some plant experiences in the areas of discipline and promotional opportunities. Allegations of lack of cooperation by workers had come from foremen who were "too busy" to explain their abrupt instructions on the floor. Bargaining unit jobs involving paperwork and reading skills were going mostly to employees who had these skills when employed. In short, the non-English-speaking Latins had become insecure and inhibited at the workplace—so much so that rather than ask the foreman to repeat his instructions, they took chances, hoping that they were right. Sometimes they were not, and the repercussions were unpleasant. A decision was made to reverse this problem by employing, at least for the summer, a full-time language instructor.

With the support of the division's executive vice-president, F. Buff, approval of the venture was achieved when it received the endorsement of Mr. Lamb, who had been appointed to coordinate the manpower development efforts of Tenneco Chemicals in March.

The scope of training responsibility. On June 23, 1969, Miss Linda Porcino, a skilled language instructor, was employed for the following purposes:

1. Instruction of the Division's New Jersey hourly workers of Latin descent in basic "industrial" English, and
2. Instruction of those among the foremen and supervisors who were non-Latin in the fundamentals of basic conversational Spanish.

Since this represented the first venture of its kind at General Foam, some rather deliberate controls were placed on the project:

1. Rather than experience various forms of trial-and-error at each of the New Jersey facilities, it was decided that Linda, after an orientation period, would spend the entire first week (June 23–27) at *one* location to make the break-in easier.
2. After this initial week, and during every second week thereafter, the Industrial Relations Department would conduct a critique of her teaching experiences with her.
3. Since Linda, too, had to find as many catalysts as possible for her effort during the relatively short time she had, she was encouraged to purchase whatever visual aids she felt necessary to conduct her classes.

4. Twice during the program, the instructor was to submit written progress reports. These would evaluate the following:
   a. Eagerness of workers and management participation.
   b. Consistency of punctuality and attendance.
   c. Methods of utilizing the diversity of skills of the workers at a given plant.
   d. Effectiveness of visual aids and textbooks.
   e. The degree to which participation by Spanish employees might be inhibited by their intense pride.
   f. Any problems caused by the use of varying Spanish vernaculars (for example, Cuban Spanish and Puerto Rican Spanish).

D. L. Perretti, Assistant Manager for Industrial Relations, and I would orient Linda as to the spirit behind the language contained in the labor contract. With these tools, she would be able to concentrate her efforts later in the program in the area of industrial communications.

It was planned, too, that care be taken to avoid having the program become too academic. To this end, each plant was to appoint a steering committee, whose first job was to develop a glossary or catalog of terms, expressions, and instructions unique to the production operations of the plants in question. A brief glance at some of the terms and expressions that appeared in the glossaries suggests how easily a literal translation would defeat the real intent:

> Watch your hands
> Hold it
> Shut it down
> Fire up the drier
> Run the material
> Fill the hopper
> Take your time
> Run the hi-lo

Get a reading on the feeler gauge
Drag line
Nose bar
Run number
Wind up
Crib
Pass

Training of management personnel. Finally, the Industrial Relations Department instructed the management personnel who were taking Spanish lessons to speak *Spanish*—no matter how "broken" or incorrect—when addressing Spanish-speaking employees. The intent here was to create an improved employer-worker rapport by way of demonstrating that the non-Latin management members were trying—and struggling—to improve their communications as well.

The Program in Operation

The experimental program was conducted through the end of August. It is well to review the development of the program as it evolved, noting the residual and side benefits that prompted the company to continue the course work on a full-time basis.

The format of the lessons. Linda learned some quick lessons during the first week—not the least of which was that the "lesson plan" traditional to the standard operating procedure of high school and elementary school teachers had to be abandoned for our purposes. One main reason was that Linda had to welcome digressions—and these came in the form of recounted experiences by the employees of their home life or jobs in the plant. Since these added a practical dimension to the teaching, they had to be accepted and, in fact, incorporated into the day's lesson.

The effect of Latin pride. Fortunately, Linda quickly became aware of the degree to which the intense Latin pride could affect the progress of her teaching. Two examples of first-day experiences in the Rockaway English classes serve to illustrate this situation.

One of the first "assignments" made by the teacher was for each student to stand and introduce himself—by relating his name, the members of his family, place of birth, and opinions about the United States as contrasted with those of the home country. After Linda had asked for a volunteer to start the ball rolling, one of the more confident class members raised his hand and declared:

> I was born in Puerto Rico. I had been passed in school all the time over there. My family lives in Puerto Rico. I came to this country two months ago. I am studying in Puerto Rico and my interest is to continue studying. I am studying in the University of Puerto Rico located in Rio Piedras, Puerto Rico. I am start to study this English class because I need the English. . . .

After complimenting the employee on his presentation, Linda asked several of the other employees for their statements. The other workers, noting that what the first student said had been accepted enthusiastically by the teacher, gave their names, then repeated the same story as told by the first student, with only minor embellishments! The only class member who had truly come to the United States two months earlier and studied at the university was the first man; but this was not as important to the others as was the matter of having their statements accepted by the teacher!

On that same day, another student had made an unusually strong oral presentation. In fact, he was known around the plant by the managers as one of the few who could speak and understand English much better than most. But later in the class, the same students were asked to *write* the presentation that they had made orally. The worker who spoke with such facility began to write:

> My family is in Puerto Rico. My father is old man. My
> father name is Juan Sanchez. In here because I want a
> learn English. Miss Porcino I want a tell you something. I
> know every word you said bot I can not write.

And with these last words, the worker—head down and obviously embarrassed—clutched his coat, went to the front of the room, thrust the paper onto the teacher's desk, and dashed out. He did not return to class, despite discreet coaxing by management.

The employee's objectives. Linda soon observed that there was little question as to what the men wanted to achieve in this course. After the first week the most representative comments from the group at Rockaway were:

1. Please speak only English in class.
2. Please correct our mistakes *as* we speak.
3. We need practice in speaking English because we find ourselves always speaking Spanish where we can.
4. We want to learn to speak better.

Participation by the employees. It was soon obvious that almost all factors affecting worker participation took on different perspectives when the classes were held on company time. Since the classes were only an hour long and involved but ten people each, this did not prove to be an unmanageable burden. But when classes were held during nonwork hours, problems of car pools and conflicts with other, private responsibilities seemed to be distracting factors.

In general, worker participation during class hours was excellent—especially when the "pride" factor was diminished by the participants' realization that they were all in the same boat. Exceptions to this were a few workers who were barely literate in Spanish *as well as* in English. It was decided that these workers should be removed from the class in favor of individual tutelage—perhaps at a time when a full-time, permanent teacher was hired. But to keep these workers in the class, as well as those who were at the other extreme (very proficient in English), it was felt, would tend to interfere with the progress of the others. We also divided the remaining class into groups based on skill in English.

The management training period. The English-to-Spanish classes proved beneficial in at least enhancing the dialog (or removing the barriers to the dialog) between the supervisors and the employees. It appeared to the employees as the purest and most tangible demonstration of management's eagerness to meet the problem halfway, using existing or available personnel, rather than hiring Spanish-speaking managers or interpreters to avoid coping with the problem.

As we had anticipated, problems of interruptions and summer vacations diminished the success of the management group's efforts. Their general unwillingness to do "homework" on a consistent basis was another negative factor. However, enough class work took place for the management learners to start noticing the similarities between the two languages and to recall key words.

Other Opportunities in the Program

Conveying information about the company. We found that the language sessions could be used as a medium for subtly conveying company intentions or programs. For example, General Foam took great pains to explain to the instructor the value to an employer of job promotions on the basis of ability and efficiency as opposed to strict seniority. This was important; rank-and-file employees are often seniority-conscious because the concept is easy to understand. For many workers, it is as simple as "first come, first served." Yet, to any sensible management, seniority is far from a guarantee that there will be accompanying skills. Therefore, we asked Linda to orient the employees accordingly. Her assistance was also enlisted to help soften the blow of lack-of-work layoffs, to design some of the printed safety material, and to prepare operating instructions.

Improvement in understanding. We have noticed that since

this program was completed, the previously mentioned human relations conferences have become much more effective. Management was hearing enough about environmental conditions in the Latin home countries so that some of the difficulties in the company began to be solved by indirect means. One example of this concerns the lunch-break controversy.

Certain shifts had 15-minute lunch periods which, although not uncommon in modern chemical industries, was resented by the Latin employees. This matter became particularly difficult, since the labor contract had been recently signed, thereby making the language binding for three years. However, it gradually emerged during the human relations meetings that the workers were not seizing upon the lunch period issue as a labor relations challenge. Rather, the problem lay in the *nature* of the midday meal. Whereas the typical American lunch is little more than a cold sandwich and coffee, often eaten "on the fly," the midday meal to the Latin is the heartiest meal of the day and, customarily, a *hot* meal. What had been happening, to the company's surprise, was that the employees' wives were preparing rice-and-beans with chicken or pork (a favorite Latin dish), which the workers were taking to the plant in large aluminum foil containers. Then, at lunchtime, all those who had brought this type of food would rush to the men's room, where an employee had brought in a hot plate with two burners. The cold rice-and-beans was then heated and doled out to whoever had brought it or would pay for a portion.

Obviously, to accomplish all this in a period of 15 minutes would be a feat worthy of praise from the best efficiency experts. The lingering indigestion provided an easy source of employee dissatisfaction. When one employee told about the clandestine hot plate activities, at one of the labor-management meetings, the following was the result:

- The company purchased for the lunchroom a large warming oven, capable of heating rice-and-beans for an entire shift.
- The company established a system whereby 15 minutes

before the lunch break, one employee was permitted to enter the lunchroom, activate the warming oven, and set up the plates and utensils. So the contract language remained intact, and the workers' 15-minute lunch period could be spent eating rather than preparing.

Some confusing problems concerning the welfare plans were also resolved at these human relations meetings. One example was the coverage for maternity. Despite the fact that the allowances were liberal, as were those in the rest of the plan, workers were complaining in a variety of ways about maternity claims. But what came to the surface as the hidden problem was entirely different.

In Puerto Rico, according to many employees, the concept of the "family physician" is not nearly as prevalent as it is in the United States. Thus when a woman who had recently arrived from Puerto Rico became pregnant, she would not have the development of this pregnancy carefully followed by a family doctor. Rather, when she felt discomfort, she would obtain medical attention from a convenient medical center one time, from a doctor recommended by a friend another time, and so forth. Thus the medical evaluation lacked the frequency, continuity, and doctor-patient rapport so important in cases such as these.

The company undertook to orient the workers to the concept of the family physician and the advantages to be gained from his use. Further, some company representatives offered to introduce families to doctors in their neighborhood who were reputable and were willing to lay the groundwork for good family-doctor relationships with those who desired it.

The company was quickly made aware that the romantic qualities among Latin men should be taken into consideration in planning for future learning programs. It was most evident that the program would be markedly less effective if the teacher were a male. This characteristic came through in a charming way in the first of two compositions written by Mr. Mercado. It was written on July 3, 1969. His last composition was written on August 20, 1969.

"My Job"

Juan Mercado
3 de Julio de 1969

Every day from Monday to Fraday I wake up at 5:30 on the morning. I start my work at 7:00 oclock. At 9:00 oclock I have coffee time and then I very working until 10:10 that I come to the lunchroom to learn more English with a nice and bautiful teacher that comes from I dont not were but really are teaching us. At 12:00 oclock I have lunch time and I start again at 12:30 and I go home at 3:30.

"My Class"

Juan Mercado
8/20/1969

My opinion about this class is the follow: the class should be longer. In that way we can learn more English and get more practice. But really the class is good, specially the way the teacher used to teach us: Reading tales, writing compositions, practicing speaking and recording our voice to see the improvement.

Evaluation of the Program

The lessons learned by the company and the benefits gained by the parties (many of these have been indirect benefits) have been so substantial that General Foam has decided to employ a language instructor on a permanent basis. It would be less than accurate to indicate that one of the more significant benefits of the ten-week experiment was the satisfactory language education of those who previously could not speak English. The time period was too short for this. Although the change in English-speaking ability among the Spanish-speaking participants was not dramatic, at least there was no longer a fear among these employees to admit that they did not understand.

It would be equally improper to indicate that by virtue of this venture, most of the company's absenteeism and turnover problems were solved. It is true that there was an improvement during this time, but much of this improvement was because of the point in the business cycle that General Foam had reached during those summer months. Indeed, the duration of the experiment and the variations imposed upon it did not lend themselves to a statistical evaluation of the results.

General Foam feels that the effect of the language program on employee relations and on relations with the union leaders has been noticeable, if only as a tangible gesture of positive intentions. Whether the value of such an approach will increase as the use of a language instructor is broadened into the areas of extended job and safety training and testing is yet to be seen.

From the point of view of Linda Porcino, however, who regrettably had to leave to return to her regular job, there was sound basis for optimism, as related in her final report:

> The success of any program of instruction depends to a large extent upon the amount of effort put forth by the students. The General Foam employees who attended the English classes regularly were not lacking in this area, clearly demonstrating their interest in improving their knowledge of English. There is no question in my mind as to the value of the program. I was able to see definite progress in the work of each student, and each one, in turn, was able to recognize his own achievement. The two Rockaway classes showed the greatest advancement for several reasons: They had more classes than did any other group (three hours, rather than two, every week); they were separated into beginning and advanced groups; they came to class during working hours and didn't have to make up this time by working another hour; and none of them had to miss classes because of vacations.
>
> Generally, all the students were sorry to see the classes come to an end, and they hope that the classes can

be resumed soon. In addition, they were sincerely appreciative of the fact that the company provided their books and dictionaries. Two men for Carlstadt, Miguel Rivera and Victorino Santiago, specifically asked me to convey their thanks to the company for the classes and the books.

The management Spanish classes were not as successful because of the fact that regular attendance was virtually impossible.

As a matter of interest you might be surprised, as I was, to learn that my Rockaway English students (the workers) gave me a Polaroid Land camera as a going-away present.

Communication is important in any training program for the disadvantaged. But when the handicaps of language and the corresponding cultural differences are also present, it is doubly incumbent on industry to take the first step, so that manager and employee can come to know and understand each other better.

A Corporate Experience:
Zale Corporation

Robert E. Williams and Abner Haynes

THE problems of working with minority groups and with undereducated, disadvantaged personnel are facing every business in America today. We feel that they are especially facing men and women in management positions.

The disadvantaged people we have taken into the Zale Corporation are part of an almost untapped source of new personnel. With a little extra effort, we are finding that hard-core unemployed can be developed into useful employees, and we believe that this can become a pattern throughout the nation.

ROBERT E. WILLIAMS is Vice-President, Personnel, Zale Corporation, Dallas, Texas.
ABNER HAYNES is Director, Equal Employment, Zale Corporation, Dallas, Texas.

Development of the Program

After we had decided to take positive action in a program to identify, recruit, hire, and train hard-core unemployed, we asked for and received federal funds under an MA-3 contract with the Department of Labor.

Abner Haynes, a well-known member of the Dallas black community and an outstanding professional athlete, was selected to be the director of the training program. His relationship with the minority groups involved provided the necessary and basic means of communication with them.

Supervisors were carefully chosen, and the new employees were placed in areas where they could receive the necessary training and supervision. Contract deadline dates forced us to enter the program before preparing the supervisors; this was done two months after the program began. Sensitivity seminars, to sharpen understanding of the behavior of others, were conducted by Mr. Haynes. The supervisors learned to exercise a degree of patience and tolerance that would not ordinarily be extended to an employee.

Prior to starting the program, meetings were held with persons in related businesses—who thus had similar problems—and with leaders in the community, to learn as much as possible about the problems of working with so-called unemployables.

Armed with this knowledge, Mr. Haynes made contacts within the ghetto areas. He visited the pool halls and bars, talked with people on street corners, and told them about our training program. As the word spread, applicants began to show up at the personnel office. They were often scared, unbelieving, and apprehensive about their chances. They were set at ease as much as possible, interviewed, and investigated to determine their eligibility to participate.

Our MA-3 training program is now completed, and we are very satisfied with the results. Our trainees are now working alongside our regular employees with only the same kind of problems common to other employees. A total of 22 persons were hired, of whom 15 are still with us.

There were several reasons for the dropouts. Some never could or would discipline themselves to come to work every day. Two were loaned money for bus fare and food and never came back. Another was outfitted with clothes and never came back to work.

Our preconceived notions about difficulties in implementing the program were for the most part substantiated. There were, however, many specific problems rooted in the particular needs of the trainees that were not known and possibly could not have been known prior to their participation in the program. The peer and supervisory relationships in work situations are examples of nonpredictable factors that influenced the project.

Most of the supervisors did not feel that they needed to know the hard-core trainee's background, although some supervisors felt strongly that if they had interviewed the trainee as they would other employees, and knew his background, this information could have been used to help in the trainee's development. Mr. Haynes, however, is convinced that telling the supervisor all of the employee's background might create prejudice or at least preferential treatment. "I'll be the counselor, you be the supervisor" is his attitude, which seems to be correct.

Polygraph tests were given by the company, however, to determine exactly what problems we were facing and if the trainee was willing to let the personnel department know about his past.

Classes were conducted at Zale on Negro history, mathematics, English, spelling, job motivation, personal hygiene, and business conduct. In addition to these subjects, the company sponsored classes in shorthand and keypunch operation at a neighboring junior college from 4:30 P.M. to 8:30 P.M., on the employee's time.

Application of the Program

In order to analyze the project and establish a picture of its status, a number of case studies will be presented. We hope they will be of some use to you in implementing your own program.

Knowledge of the employee's current personal problems is extremely important, because they affect and usually interfere with his job; in addition, he may not be mature enough to recognize the interference, nor disciplined enough to correct it. If one is aware of the problems from the outset, counseling is more effective. At Zale, when instances arose relating to the trainee's personal problems, the conversation would be directed so that he could appraise his problem and decide on the best steps to take to solve it. Most of the problems of the disadvantaged are personal, and most of these can be discovered when visiting the home. Home visitation was of major importance to us, at least in the beginning stages of our program.

An example of a real problem that we experienced involved an 18-year-old trainee who had been a "job hopper" and who had a police theft record. Through counseling, Abner Haynes learned that there was also an in-law problem. The mother of the trainee's 16-year-old wife resented the young man and came to pick up her daughter while he was at work. Often he would stay home to keep his wife at home. It was thus obvious that there were two difficulties here: (1) the money problem, because he had not been working, and (2) the in-law problem that he was neither mature nor disciplined enough to handle. Counseling provided the young man with the insight to correct his problems, and he has since become a satisfactory employee and has received a salary merit increase.

Another example involved a Mexican American who had a criminal record and who was thus considered unemployable. He was on ten years' probation and had been arrested for loitering when the police contacted Mr. Haynes to see if he could be hired. We expected that this young man would be difficult to train and that it would require time to convince him that the

130

company really wanted to help him. At the same time he needed to understand that others were depending on him to carry out his responsibilities. Mr. Haynes insisted that he break off all relationships with certain people. Counseling revealed that the criminal record related to a personal problem, which he has since overcome. He too has become a satisfactory employee and has received a salary merit increase.

Elizabeth Thompson* has been an outstanding student and participant in the training program. She began her work in July 1968 in the mail room and was soon transferred to the credit and collection department. At first she was not pleased about the change. She was frightened because she did not know her new associates or what was expected of her. She accepted the challenge of working in the credit and collection department, however, because the opportunity to learn to use the machines and to work with figures seemed more interesting to her than the work in the mail room. According to her supervisor, Miss Thompson has made excellent progress. The supervisor found that an understanding, but not patronizing, attitude toward her was effective in helping her feel at ease in the department; this in turn helped her to become a more productive employee. The classes referred to earlier were a definite morale booster for her. She had not thought that such an opportunity would be available when she joined the company.

We might also mention that when Miss Thompson joined the credit and collection department, she was the only black person in an all-white department. Situations similar to this are apt to occur when the total number of hard-core employed is not large. It is thus particularly incumbent on all others in a department to help a disadvantaged employee feel comfortable when he or she has no one else there to identify with.

Supervisors in the accounting department are very pleased with the work performance of their four disadvantaged employees. Fellow workers trained the employees, and each trainee has been assigned a project for which he is responsible.

* All names of hard-core trainees used in this article are fictitious.

Learning to operate the machines and to work with figures have been a challenge. One of the individuals requested a more difficult task and has executed the job well. (The supervisors boast that one employee ranked first in the shorthand class.)

Two disadvantaged employees have worked in the traffic department, and their supervisor is well pleased with their work. The supervisor has noticed a lack of competence in the use of business machines; however, he feels that with six more months of experience in the office the employees will be ready for an advanced class in transportation.

A company executive hired a temporary clerk during the Christmas rush. He recalls that when he asked her when she would be ready to go to work she sat quietly for ten seconds and then began to cry, "Are you really going to hire me? I didn't think you would; nobody else will." She proved to be extraordinarily dependable and became a full-time employee.

Later another full-time employee was hired in the same department. She required great assistance. She was bitter, and her work and attendance at previous jobs were sporadic. Since she has participated in our program, however, her dress, hair, and makeup have improved. She is bright, has made many friends, and is good for department morale. When she works for the executives personally, she takes great pains to be accurate, and becomes very upset if she makes a mistake. She has been given financial assistance (which she is paying back through payroll deduction) as well as moral support after having been hospitalized. "It has been necessary to walk an extra mile with her, but that is the purpose of the program, and that is exactly what you would do if she were a member of your family," said Mr. Haynes. The "last-chance effort" seemed to be what she needed. Her supervisor told her after she had been absent and late a great deal that "the single most important thing she was to think about before going to sleep was that she must get up and come to her job in the morning, never to be late again." She was pleased that someone cared enough about her to tell her that she was needed; apparently she needed the direction.

The construction department purchases a large volume of supplies from many sources before completing construction. A trainee has been assisting with the many details and is gradually learning more. It is easy to confuse him, but when he is given one job at a time until he learns it, he can be very helpful.

Data processing has been an experimental area because its employees have always been pretrained. One of our hard-core trainees, Mr. Jenkins, has been learning from the other employees and has gradually undertaken duties in this area. He had an absenteeism problem, which was alleviated by setting short-range goals with associated rewards. During the period of absenteeism, Mr. Haynes and the supervisor decided that a salary increase for Mr. Jenkins should be postponed. An arrangement was then worked out with his supervisor whereby Mr. Jenkins would be assigned a regular job if he came to work, on time, for six consecutive weeks. He did this and has received a raise. He also has been working overtime; this is an indication of his progress, because overtime wages would not be paid if he were not productive. His supervisor reports that he should be ready to enroll in data processing classes after another 12 to 18 months of on-the-job training.

Conclusions and Recommendations

In summary, our conclusions and recommendations are as follows:

1. Prepare and select foremen and managers to accept the disadvantaged employee into their work situation as they would any new employee, but recognize the special attention and support required.
2. Plan an initial and follow-up training and educational program for each disadvantaged employee.
3. Select candidates for the program on a broad prerequisite basis within predetermined limits. As experience and knowledge of the program develop, the limits

should be extended to include cases involving greater risk.

4. Provide for counseling services for each trainee. The counselors will wean the employee from themselves and transfer to the supervisor whatever dependence is required (not unlike the usual new employee).

5. Loans and gifts of money will create insurmountable problems in most cases. Care must be exercised in this area. In all cases a plan should be established for repayment by the trainees from their own resources.

6. Lateness, absenteeism, and rules infractions should not be overlooked or neglected. Prompt action on these matters helps the employee to learn responsibility and the need to comply with company policy.

7. Educate and train all employees, at all levels, in sensitivity, communication, problem-solving techniques, understanding, and caring.

The success of the hard-core training program can best be attested to by our obtaining a second contract, MA-4, in which we have hired 120 trainees in eight cities across the nation. We plan to continue to assist in the development of minority groups in major cities throughout the country.

A Corporate Experience:
American Airlines

Robert H. Gudger

Long before the National Alliance of Businessmen (NAB) launched its program to provide training for the hard-core unemployed, American Airlines had participated in on-the-job training (OJT) projects in this area in three cities. Our experiences at that time provided a meaningful framework for ensuing programs.

Having successfully demonstrated—in Los Angeles, Buffalo, and Chicago—our ability to train and absorb so-called unemployables, we moved to develop an MA-3 program under the NAB. We had to analyze our employment needs, examine our internal capabilities, and determine the financial commitment necessary to implement our moral commitment.

ROBERT H. GUDGER is Manager, Employee Relations, American Airlines, Inc.

Development of the Program

Job classifications. American Airlines is a medium-size corporation with about 35,000 employees and an average yearly separation turnover of about 5.9 percent. In our annual review of hiring practices regarding the disadvantaged, we narrowed the forecast of new employees to only three or four categories. We eliminated specific jobs on the basis of any or all of the following reasons:

- Requirement of college or advanced degrees.
- A training period of at least a year.
- Little or no turnover in classification (this would allow for fewer trainees).
- Too extensive equipment needs.

Therefore we decided to train and employ in the following four classifications:

1. Fleet service clerks (cargo and cabin service maintenance men).
2. Aircraft cleaners.
3. Building cleaners.
4. Stock and parts clerks.

The number of trainees. While examining classifications, we were also considering the number to be trained. We had no intention of merely trying to look good to the government. We wanted to place trainees in meaningful employment. Thus we had to be sure that the number of trainees agreed upon would in fact have jobs at the completion of training and would be freed from the fear that "the last hired would be the first fired."

One further point had to be reviewed: whether to develop an initial proposal for one city served by the company with expansion a year later, or to propose participation in a number of cities and thereby accommodate more trainees.

The final decision was based to a large extent on the company's commitment to reduce tensions in urban centers. Recognizing that unemployment, underemployment, and lack of training are more than just symptoms of urban disease, we saw that one important cure would be to provide training and jobs at wages above the poverty level. As a result, we decided to initially train and employ 350 "unemployables" in ten cities. The number of trainees in each city would be based on need—bearing in mind the starting dates of the program requirement, the need to complete training within a year, and the necessity that a specific job exist at the completion of training.

Initially, all 50 cities having American Airlines facilities were contacted. Each submitted a report forecasting new employees for the year in the four job categories named previously, and indicating the locale's general interest in the program. Careful analysis of the reports provided information sufficient to decide on ten cities—and the 350 target figure. The following criteria were used to determine the number of disadvantaged trainees by location. The number was

1. Not to exceed 1.1 percent of total company employees.
2. Not to exceed 15 percent (preferably less than 10 percent) of the total number of people in the job classification in the given location.
3. Not to exceed 25 percent of the new employees in the job classification in a particular location.
4. Limited to 10 locations from 50 major cities designated by the federal government.

A detailed job category breakdown by locale is shown in Exhibit 1.

Acceptance and initiation. The proposal that had been accepted by the corporation and the field offices was submitted to the Labor Department for approval. Upon notification of final approval, we put the wheels in motion for starting the program in the ten cities.

Each city was requested to appoint a coordinator and a counselor/coach on the basis of the criteria contained in the contract proposal. In the meantime, bids for subcontracting orientation and skill training were already being reviewed. A systemwide meeting was arranged for all coordinators, counselors, and representatives of line management to work out final details, including tentative starting dates, and to review procedures for recruitment, sensitivity training, and evaluation.

Organizational structure for implementation and control. Since responsibility to the U.S. Department of Labor rested

Exhibit 1

Job Category Breakdown by Locale

Locale	Fleet Service Clerks	Air- craft Clean- ers	Build- ing Clean- ers	Stock and Parts Clerks	Total Commit- ment
Boston	9	1	—	—	10
Cleveland	6	1	—	—	7
Chicago	63	7	2	—	72
Los Angeles	24	14	2	—	40
San Francisco	15	3	1	—	19
Dallas/Fort Worth	15	2	—	—	17
Detroit	25	2	—	—	27
Washington, D.C.	9	3	—	—	12
New York—John F. Kennedy International Airport	28	7	1	—	36
New York—La- Guardia Airport	30	1	6	—	37
Newark, N.J.	6	1	1	—	8
Tulsa Maintenance and Engineering Center	—	—	—	65	65
Total	230	42	13	65	
Total no. of trainees					350

with our corporate headquarters, central control had to be established on a systemwide basis. Although each city could develop its own specific timetable for training (including such things as number of sessions and class size), corporate head-

138

quarters would coordinate efforts of the ten cities and report directly to the Labor Department. This would insure consistency in curriculum design and content. Each city would select a coordinator and a counselor/coach. The system coordinator would report to the personnel department. However, each field or local coordinator would report to a local line officer in keeping with our overall organizational structure. This was to insure the line personnel's support of the program and of the trainees. The coordinator would administer the program, while the counselor/coach would have direct responsibility for the needs of the trainee, through all phases of the program—from orientation to final follow-up and evaluation.

Sensitivity training would be developed by company trainers with support from the subcontractor but ultimately would be conducted on a continuing basis by each counselor/coach with consultative support from the corporate training department. The counselor/coach would in time be expected to develop a knowledge of the needs of supervisors and employees for such training.

Standards for Training

The training personnel. With a national program for implementation in ten cities, the question arose as to *who* would conduct the training. Since the decisions to proceed involved the inputs of line supervisors as well as our corporate group, our training and development department called upon line instructors for their recommendations.

In addition, we had learned from our previous OJT projects that although our instructors would serve as backup, their other assignments would preclude their availability on a full-time, ongoing basis. Therefore, orientation and prevocational training was subcontracted to outside professionals. However, the sensitivity training for supervisors, managers, and workers was assigned initially to our own training personnel, both line and staff. In time, however, this was increasingly shared with outside professionals.

Criteria for trainee selection. As we finished plans for the actual training program design, we consulted with first-line supervisors and instructors and developed a week-by-week timetable whereby a trainee could become a full-time, regular employee. We reviewed with them the "profile" of the trainee we would be accepting in the program. Our criteria paralleled those of the federal government, which are as follows:

Poor persons without suitable employment who are
1. School dropouts.
2. Under 22 years of age.
3. Forty-five years of age or over.
4. Handicapped.
5. Subject to special obstacles to employment—that is,
   (a) Unskilled.
   (b) Unemployed.
   (c) Underemployed.
   (d) Having a family history of welfare support.
   (e) Laid off from declining industries.
   (f) Members of minority groups.

After careful review and analysis of previous programs, we agreed that the equivalent of an eighth-grade education was necessary to perform adequately in the job classifications decided upon. We learned from our experience in Los Angeles, Buffalo, and Chicago that after six to ten weeks of intensive training, an individual initially functioning at a fourth- or fifth-grade level could qualify for high school equivalency or at least function at an eighth- to ninth-grade level. Thus we outlined a plan of training as follows:

Stage	Activity	Time period
Phase I	Recruitment	Variable
Phase II	Job orientation	2 weeks
Phase III	Prevocational training	6 weeks
Phase IV	On-the-job training	12 weeks
Phase V	Follow-up and evaluation	No time limit

It was further decided that all training (including job orientation and prevocational training) would be conducted in the job area itself in order to familiarize the trainees with their work locations. Classrooms would be selected near actual work sites, and part of each session would be spent away from the classroom, on the work site itself.

Financial Considerations

Although most NAB/JOBS program costs were reimbursable, we saw the need to project the company's costs beyond those to be reimbursed by the government. Our initial budget proposal therefore included auxiliary services, the cost of which would be totally borne by the company. These included the following:

- Medical examinations, including basic exam costs and corrective costs for items such as eyeglasses.
- Transportation, to compensate trainees when public transportation is inadequate.
- Licenses and fees, for driver's licenses and driver training, when necessary.
- Initial lunch and emergency funds for trainees during their initial eight weeks of training.

Over a two-year period for 350 trainees per year, these costs were expected to total approximately $240,000. (We had also projected costs for training 250 or 150 employees. See Exhibit 2.) Our chairman of the board recommended the $240,000 expenditure to the Board of Directors, indicating that this would represent the company's financial commitment to the NAB/JOBS program. Board approval was immediate and unanimous.

We decided to limit publicity on the program for the first year, and to mesh training dates with peak employment periods to avoid employing trainees above budget. Again, we wanted to avoid "last hired, first fired" situations.

Exhibit 2

Projected Training Costs

	350 Trainees	250 Trainees	150 Trainees
Wages @ $1,000 per trainee	$350,000	$250,000	$150,000
Trainee benefits @ $100 per trainee	35,000	25,000	15,000
Administration and other direct and indirect costs	227,000	210,000	196,000
Subcontract training @ $500 per trainee	175,000	125,000	75,000
Cost of total commitment	$787,000	$610,000	$436,000
Cost per trainee	$ 2,250	$ 2,440	$ 2,900
Reimbursement by contract per trainee			
Maximum anticipated	$ 2,250	$ 2,250	$ 2,250
Minimum anticipated	$ 1,400	$ 1,400	$ 1,400
OJT productivity @ 50% per trainee	$ 265	$ 265	$ 265
Cost to company under minimum reimbursement per trainee	$ 585	$ 775	$ 1,235
Total commitment	$240,750	$193,750	$185,250

Agreements with the Union

With this support of our basic proposal, we met with officers of the union and reached the following agreements regarding training and subsequent employment:

1. The disadvantaged trainees are not to be subject to the company-union agreement until after they have been certified as fully qualified and productive in a specific classification.
2. The trainees are not to displace or perform the work normally assigned to the employee in the classification.

3. The trainees are to be assigned to a designated supervisor, in order to give each trainee a single source of guidance and counsel and to make readily ascertainable a supervisory evaluation of the trainee's progress or lack of progress. In addition, if the trainee follows the designated supervisor from one shift to another, this would discourage the claim that the trainee is working a shift or has days off that should be opened for bid by our regular employees.
4. When a trainee is certified as fully qualified in the appropriate classification, his probationary period starts with the first workday following the certification. At this time he will be subject to the company-union agreement just as any new employee normally is.

Implementation Guidelines

The basic criteria for hiring and training the disadvantaged had been established by the Department of Labor. In addition, however, we had to develop our own guidelines on the basis of the requirements of the jobs involved.

Standards in hiring. First, we decided to refer to the men as "JOBS trainees," to avoid placing an additional stigma on individuals who were already victims of vicious stereotyping.

Analysis of our four job classifications indicated that a trainee would have to meet the following basic standards:

1. Trainability at least to an eighth-grade level, and preferably to high school level.
2. Possession of or capability of obtaining a motor vehicle operator's license.
3. Tolerance for working around noise and at considerable heights.
4. Standard preemployment medical examination.
5. Indication of an interest in employment in this partic-

ular industry (during or after a tour of the company's facilities). (In previous OJT programs, we found a definite correlation between the trainee's interest in the industry and his eventual success.)

Procedures in recruitment. These had to be expanded to include CEP (Concentrated Employment Programs) and the U.S. Employment Service, as well as numerous minority referral sources under the Office of Economic Opportunity (OEO) and agencies such as the Urban League. Since traditional methods probably would not be adequate, we established a procedure for recruitment and selection of trainees, to be coordinated with agencies certified by CEP to refer the disadvantaged. We felt that even better results would be obtained by recruiting and selecting in the inner city, preferably at the site of the referral agency. All preliminary screening, application filing, and evaluation would also be conducted at that site. Subsequent contacts could be conducted at the company facility, but by that time, some rapport would have been established with the prospective trainee. Information about police records, narcotics use, and welfare status could be openly discussed. Further, the agency would be able to maintain contact with any applicants not accepted. After these preliminaries, interested applicants could be given a tour of the company facility, including the work area—in some cases, even at night to simulate conditions on the shift to which trainees would probably be assigned. In addition, the applicant's tolerance of the noise factor and working heights could be judged. A trainee would be eligible for selection upon successfully completing a medical examination. All testing would be performed after acceptance—usually on the first day of work, along with orientation.

The recruitment process takes approximately one week from the time of first contact with the trainee. Our philosophy in this process has been to screen-in applicants, not screen them out. We have made it clear to referral agencies that it is not necessary for us to screen 50 applicants if we are seeking 10 trainees for a particular class. We prefer to see as few applicants as possible—with little or no education, with police records or other employment handicaps. We seek the poorest prospects, not the best of the worst.

When the prospective trainee is being processed either by the recruiter or in the firm's personnel department, it is important to remember the following:

- Remove items such as arrest records, and any other items that could be discriminatory in nature, from the application forms.
- Don't permit a receptionist or clerk to make decisions about screening candidates, unless the receptionist or clerk has been properly trained.
- Eliminate all testing where possible. If it is necessary to retain tests, be sure that they are validated in terms of the work to be performed.
- Don't make it necessary for the applicants to see several persons before a hiring decision is made.
- Try to minimize the time spent between initial contact and final selection.

Criminal or narcotics records. To be consistent throughout our ten cities, we have established certain guidelines for accepting trainees with criminal or narcotics records. If the prospective trainee has been arrested but not convicted—regardless of the crime—or arrested and convicted of a misdemeanor, his acceptance is within the local coordinator's discretion. If arrested and convicted of a felony, he needs general office clearance. Conviction or arrest for possession of marijuana is acceptable, as is arrest for possession of heroin—except if convicted. A "pusher" of narcotics of any type is not accepted. After selection for training, narcotics users receive only one warning during the eight-week orientation and skill training period, and are dropped immediately during OJT. Decisions regarding addicts are made by American's medical staff.

Additional standards. We also set out other guidelines regarding dismissal of trainees during various phases of the training. Both ideally and realistically, we are prepared to allow greater flexibility and allowances in the early stages of training. Once a trainee reaches the on-the-job training phase, however, he must conform to normal company standards. In essence, he is given eight weeks to develop the required sense of responsibility regarding his job. We remain committed to avoiding a double standard once the trainee becomes a full-time union employee. This was a joint decision with the union. Assimilation of trainees into the workforce is clearly easier and more acceptable to present employees in this context.

The Trainee in the Company

A common pitfall in training programs is the tendency to choose careers for the trainees. When this occurs, the program will not succeed, simply because the trainees were not allowed to select their own areas of training on the basis of their interests, abilities, and career aspirations.

The job that the trainee ultimately assumes should allow him a degree of authority and responsibility in that position. To assign him a task that merely "fills a slot," with no real prospects for the future, would be a waste of his newly acquired skills.

Explanation of the job structure. In order to enable an applicant to select a particular job intelligently, all aspects of the work must be fully explained to him. This should include information about the job site and the organizational structure in which he will function. Reporting relationships should be outlined carefully. Ultimately a review of his needs in light of the job should be made. In addition, the team aspect of employment should be emphasized. The intercorrelation of functions and the absence of isolated functions should be stressed. In this way, the trainee will realize that his assignment is a vital one because it fits in the total process of running a company.

The supervisors' role. If a program to train the unemployed or underemployed is to succeed, supervisors should be involved in the planning stages. It is not enough, however, merely to sensitize first-level supervisors. All levels of management should be made aware of the program and be given sensitivity training. This involves more than just communication of the company's commitment from the top down. It means taking the time to give definitive information and to provide an opportunity for open and frank dialog. A continuing forum for discussion should be included in any such program. Introducing the trainee to his supervisors and co-workers should be accomplished as normally as possible. Don't overstate the case—that is, be careful not to go to such lengths that fear or apprehension will arise in the mind of the supervisor about the trainee. It is up to the supervisor to introduce the trainee to his co-workers. In addition, the supervisor should set aside some time for briefing the trainee about his job assignment. This briefing should include an explanation of reporting relationships, especially as to who "gives orders" when he is not around.

The "buddy" system. One individual from the workforce who indicates some interest in the program should be teamed up with a particular trainee. This "buddy" should be responsible for assisting the trainee in working into the unit and for any personal affairs, such as employee activities, banking, or credit unions. When counselors are used, some of the "buddy's" functions can be shared.

Follow-up procedures. Through the process outlined above, it will be possible to evaluate a trainee's assimilation. Feedback can be obtained from the "buddy," as well as from the trainee's supervisor and counselor. In addition, the need for upgrading skills can be recognized and implemented, but until the trainee really feels comfortable in the company, it is not feasible to treat him like just another employee. A trainee is likely to indicate that he is a full member of the team by his performance.

The Results—Statistically

Statistically—and judging from observations and the opinions of those directly involved—American's NAB/JOBS program has been a success. The retention ratio bears this out. The feelings of supervisors about trainees substantiate it. The attitudes of trainees retained prove the point best of all. As one trainee phrased it, "This program not only gave me a chance to prove I was equal, but even to be better than someone else."

That the overall retention rate for JOBS trainees (64.9 percent) is higher than that for normal new employees (59.9 percent) is significant. (The NAB national retention percentage for the same period is 55.8 percent.) Our retention percentage is higher when terminations beyond the company's control, such as subsequent medical problems and drafts into military service, are excluded (see Exhibit 3).

Exhibit 3

Retention Rates in Program After 18 Months

| | | Retention Rates | |
Locale	Total No. of Trainees in Program	All Reasons (Percent)	Controllable Reasons Only (Percent)
Boston	24	66.7	79.2
Chicago	60	66.7	75.0
Cleveland	16	63.5	81.3
Dallas/Fort Worth	29	65.6	75.9
Detroit	39	38.5	69.3
Los Angeles	43	72.1	81.4
New York (JFK and La-Guardia Airports) and Newark, N.J.	88	62.5	79.5
San Francisco	25	72.0	76.0
Tulsa Maintenance and Engineering Center	71	83.1	88.4
Washington, D.C.	24	58.4	75.0
Total	419	Avg. 64.9	82.1

By isolating the "controllable" reasons we can better deal with them in future training classes—and hopefully reduce their occurrence. We are presently conducting taped follow-up interviews with unsuccessful trainees to establish whether it was the trainee or the trainer—the company—who was actually "unsuccessful."

Other data that we developed about the trainees indicated the following: average family size, 3.9 persons; average education, grade 10.4; unemployment average, 25.4 weeks; family income for the preceding year per trainee (retained or not), $2,773; average age, 25; known police record, 55 percent; black trainees, 72 percent.

Other Conclusions

Statistics are not enough, however. They do not tell *why* we feel the program to date has been so successful. Perhaps the fundamental reason was simply that our counselors, coordinators, and instructors proved to each trainee that he was important to us, that we truly cared about him. Other factors included the following:

- The jobs for which the hard core were being trained were entry-level and not dead-end. Definite advancement possibilities existed, and the trainees were made aware of these early in the program. In a few instances, trainees have been promoted to jobs several levels above the entry job. This has created an even greater incentive to other trainees. But it is still too soon to evaluate how rapidly JOBS trainees advance compared to normal new employees.
- Dropping the label "hard-core trainees" and substituting the title of "JOBS trainees" helped the men to view themselves in a better light and conditioned others to see them less negatively.

- The trainee knew—from the day he was selected for training—that he had a job, and was not merely training for a job. Too often, programs have provided training without relation to specific openings. When no job develops, the trainee is simply left with another failure and disappointment to live with.
- The basic skills training curriculum was designed to provide the trainee with qualifications beyond those necessary for his immediate job. This insured that he met the minimum requirements for the job; it also encouraged supervisors to seek out the trainees, not just accept them or be "saddled" with them.
- Moving the trainee through three pay grades gave him a sense of achievement. True, we were using the reward system, but when the trainee was shown that he could accomplish something tangible, he developed a sense of worth and confidence in himself and confidence in the value of learning.
- Classrooms located close to his actual work area enabled the trainee to readily observe, and become accustomed to, activities he would soon be engaged in. His instructors and counselors regularly gave him time to see what was going on. He had an incentive to get out there and work. Also, many of the activities being performed by regular employees were included in his training. Thus he learned by doing. His training became relevant—and so did he.
- Counselors paid close attention to seemingly insignificant personal problems of the trainee. ("Do you have lunch money?" "Is your transportation working out?" "How is your family?") By anticipating the minor needs of trainees, we headed off or minimized major personal crises.

Overall, we have been able to help each successful trainee *become* motivated—simply by removing or eliminating the demotivating factors that had engulfed him.

In addition, we have learned, perhaps above all else, that empathy, not sympathy, is essential. We have cautioned our instructors and counselors about getting too close to the trainees. Overidentification from either side could lead to greater dependence, rather than instilling confidence and independence. Most of all, we have learned a good deal about ourselves as supervisors, managers, counselors, and human beings. We have learned to cope with new situations. We have enlarged the scope of our knowledge and of our interpersonal relationships. We have also learned some rather basic things:

1. Counseling forms the core of the program. We have to prepare the trainee psychologically for the world of work. We must help him to eliminate outside worries so he can concentrate on learning. We must make learning relevant and mix it with "doing" to increase his attention span.

2. We encourage company employees (black and Spanish-American employees particularly) to visit classes and talk to trainees. When possible, pilots or flight officers, agents, or management personnel also visit. This provides identification with someone meaningful, a "role model" all too often lacking in the trainee's "other world."

3. Intangibles are important to the trainee: the satisfaction of taking home a paycheck and opening a bank account; the feeling of earning while learning; the sense of accomplishment that comes from working with two or three other fellows to complete a task.

The "flightseeing" trip we provide for trainees at the end of their 12-week program—often to a city two or three thousand miles away—gives them something to look forward to and to work toward.

We have learned, too, that trainees can learn faster and can reach higher levels of achievement than was first assumed. Therefore, we are looking at more sophisticated job classifications and are considering accepting trainees at grade levels below fifth or sixth.

We have encountered some problems with trainees reporting to shifts—especially late-night shifts. Often, we have failed to fully cover details about such work. (For example, the employee goes to our "ready room," looks at a worksheet for his name, and is assigned three or four aircraft to work on. The supervisor is often elsewhere; other employees are scurrying to their assignments. Getting to unfamiliar gates where aircraft arrive is not altogether easy. Little wonder that a trainee can get confused!)

We have learned that a "buddy" system, especially during the on-the-job phase, helps overcome some problems that usually arise after classroom training. Fortunately, the union allows the "buddy" a few hours a week to help the trainee become adjusted. We see in this a sign that union commitment to the JOBS concept is getting even stronger.

A Nine-Step Approach

If you are contemplating undertaking training the hardcore unemployed, we suggest that you take a look once more at our course of action. The following nine-step approach to a government-supported program will help any industry to better provide meaningful employment:

1. Choose government programs carefully. Investigate them all.
2. Set up a chain of command, in writing, from the top down, for the implementation of the program. Budget for costs over available reimbursements.
3. Bring in first-level supervisors early; provide continual sensitivity training for all levels of management.
4. Start with entry-level jobs. Make room at the bottom by upgrading some of the employees now at the bottom. Waive high school requirements and arrest-record limitations.

5. Examine the feasibility of meshing the program with existing training programs.
6. Coordinate the program with your regular employment processes, including application taking, testing criteria, and assignment procedures.
7. Be flexible and realistic about steps 1 to 6. Do not be discouraged by failure of some aspect of the program. Try another approach. Review hiring procedures for flaws. Evaluate testing programs—or eliminate them.
8. Centralize responsibility for the program. If this is not feasible, assign liaison personnel for implementation.
9. Periodically monitor the progress of the program and of the trainees.

A Final Word

These are some of the major requisites for any concerted attack on the massive unemployment faced by the disadvantaged. There has always been a gap between the unemployed or underemployed on the one hand and industry and organized labor on the other because of the color barrier. Today, with poor education, lack of skills, and little hope superimposed on color and poverty, the gap has been widened. Immediate action is needed from industry and labor.

Industry has the know-how, the leverage, and the resources to do the job. It spends billions of dollars on research; indeed, directors and managers are characteristically very venturesome in research programs. But they hesitate to use non-traditional methods in recruiting, hiring, training, and upgrading blacks and other members of disadvantaged groups.

Today's unemployed and underemployed cannot be helped by gradual changes in education alone. However, government programs now available can help these people and help business. Don't fall into the trap of merely saying that blacks and other disadvantaged need to be motivated, for, more fundamentally, the need is to remove the demotivators that permeate our society.

The biggest mistake industry can make with regard to unemployment, training, poverty, and discrimination is to ignore them, or make little of them, or do nothing about them. Then these problems will become insurmountable.